BOOKS BY ELLA E. CLARK

Poetry: An Interpretation of Life
(New York, 1935)
Indian Legends of the Pacific Northwest
(Berkeley, 1953)
Indian Legends of Canada
(Toronto, 1960)
Indian Legends from the Northern Rockies
(Norman, 1966)
Guardian Spirit Quest
(Billings, 1974)
In the Beginning
(Billings, 1977)

Sacagawea of the Lewis and Clark Expedition

Sacagawea sculpture, Bismarck, North Dakota, by
Leonard Crunelle (1910). Photo: State Historical Society
of North Dakota.

Sacagawea of the Lewis and Clark Expedition

*Ella E. Clark and
Margot Edmonds*

University of California Press
Berkeley · Los Angeles · London

Contents

Acknowledgments   vii
Prologue   1
Part I. The Expedition   5

   1. Jefferson's Dream   7
   2. Sacagawea Joins the Expedition   14
   3. Sacagawea on the Jefferson River   22
   4. Journey Over the Rockies   32
   5. Down Three Rivers to the Pacific   39
   6. Winter at Fort Clatsop   49
   7. Eastward Bound   59
   8. The Explorers Separate   69
   9. The Explorers Reunite and Return   78

Part II. Sacagawea in Historical Perspective   85

  10. Nearly a Century of Neglect   87
  11. A Legend Begins: Sacagawea Becomes "the Guide"   93
  12. Sacagawea, a Controversial Figure   103
  13. Some of Eastman's Discoveries   113
  14. Sacagawea on the Wind River Reservation   122
  15. Finn Burnett's Recollections of Sacagawea 132
  16. The Aged Sacagawea   140

Appendix A Pronunciation of Indian Names   147
Appendix B Sources   150
Appendix C Indian Children's Story   153
Appendix D Sacagawea Memorials   155
Notes and Additional Information   159
Bibliography: Books and Manuscripts   163
Index   167

Acknowledgments

To those who have assisted in gathering the material and to others who have helped to improve the presentation of it, we wish to express our appreciation publicly:

To Eugenia Langford, of the Library of the Department of the Interior, who really prompted this long study. At the end of my three months of research in the Smithsonian Institution and in the public libraries of Washington, D. C. (part of my preparation for my second and third collections of Indian myths and legends), Mrs. Langford gave me a copy of the long letter that Dr. Charles Eastman wrote to the Commissioner of Indian Affairs on March 2, 1925, summarizing his study of "Sacajawea of the Wind River Reservation," Wyoming.

To Jane Smith and Richard C. Crawford, of the National Archives and Records Service, for sending a microfilm copy of almost all of "the sworn testimonies" made to Eastman by Shoshone Indians and by two white men in Wyoming, by a Hidatsa (Minnetaree) woman at Fort Berthold, North Dakota, and by three Comanche Indians of Oklahoma. Eastman's reports had been transferred to the National Archives from the Bureau of Indian Affairs.

To David Crosson, Research Librarian, Western History Research Center, University of Wyoming, for a copy of the letters from Tom Rivington to Grace Hebard.

To Nancy Carlock, formerly a librarian, and to Aline Kegley, formerly a teacher of literature, for reading my manuscript at different stages and giving me both helpful criticism and encouragement.

To Margot Edmonds, who was so very helpful with the improvement of troublesome parts in the manuscript that I invited her to be my co-author.

To Virginia Langdon, Editorial Consultant, who wrote, "Because of the importance of the book, I took more than my usual time for reading"—and preceded her compliments with nearly nine type-written pages of helpful critical suggestions!

To Doctor Albert W. Thompson, retired professor and retired Dean of the Humanities at Washington State University, for his suggestions of recent books on my subjects and of very important articles in recent issues of Northwest historical journals and, later, for his critical reading of the manuscript (Part II twice).

E.E.C.

To Elizabeth D. Woodbury, Reference Librarian of the Department of the Interior, for her suggestions of where to find monuments, memorials, and honors to Sacagawea.

To the Historical Societies of Montana, Wyoming, Idaho, Utah, North Dakota, South Dakota, Washington, and Oregon for valuable help in the location of memorials to Sacagawea and for photographic illustrations.

M.E.

To the University of California Press editorial staff with special plaudits to Ron Cooney, copy editor.

E.E.C. and M.E.

Prologue

Sacajawea has become a national heroine; there are more statues to her than to any other American woman.

Colliers Encyclopedia (1976)

Madonna of her race, she had led the way to a new time. To the hands of this girl, not yet eighteen, had been entrusted the key that unlocked the road to Asia.

Eva Emery Dye, *The Conquest:*
The True Story of Lewis and Clark

For one hundred and seventy-five years there have been two Sacagaweas. Called by many "the guide" of the Lewis and Clark Expedition, the fictional Sacagawea has been portrayed as a woman whose abilities as a scout and trailblazer were outstripped only by her physical beauty and unspoken commitment to manifest destiny. Of course, Sacagawea's involvement in what was a superhuman undertaking is the stuff of which myths are made, and the story of the teen-aged Shoshone girl single-handedly guiding a large expedition through unexplored territory is irresistible fiction if inaccurate history. Descriptions like that of Eva Emery Dye have helped to burnish a popular image that can still be found in both fictional and historical accounts of the Lewis and Clark Expedition.

In truth, the legend obscures both the person and the very real contributions Sacagawea made to the first organized, scientific exploration of the American West, contributions which assured the success of the Expedition and which no one else could have performed. With her infant son strapped to her back most of the time, Sacagawea was a member of the main party from April 7, 1805, until August 14, 1806. In that time she shared the explorers' many hardships and their few pleasures.

It is the aim of this biography to place Sacagawea's life and accomplishments in historical perspective, and to dispel the fog of idolatry which has surrounded her for so long. Our intention is not, as might be supposed, to depreciate what she did or to lessen her role in the Lewis and Clark Expedition. On the contrary, we hope to *emphasize* her importance by plainly stating the part she played in a historic feat. We hope also to present a clear picture of her character and of her life *after* the exploration, a subject which has been examined very little. Through these means, we intend to draw a factual and not idealized portrait of a remarkable woman who was (and *is*) no less of a national heroine for having been at the same time a human being.

Our book is divided into two parts. The first tells the story of Sacagawea's role in the Lewis and Clark Expedition, based largely on the accounts given in the journals of the explorers, with information culled from other sources where it is appropriate, including personal interviews. We briefly sketch the beginnings of the Expedition for those whose memories of this phase of history may be dim, and we give a chronological report of the Expedition's progress, with emphasis on the episodes where Sacagawea played an important part. Because there are few factual records of Sacagawea's day-by-day participation in the Expedition, we occasionally must speculate on her activities, but such speculation is always based on authentic information.

The second part extends the story of Sacagawea past the time of the Expedition, and we can certify that she lived to an old age and died in 1884. Much of Part II is based on the recorded testimonies of Dr. Charles Eastman, a Sioux Indian, who investigated the life and death of Sacagawea in 1924 at the request of the Commissioner of Indian Affairs. The summary of his testimonies lay virtually unknown in the National Archives until one of us (E.E.C.) was fortuitously prompted to examine the documents.

The main sources of additional information are the *Original Journals of the Lewis and Clark Expedition, 1804–1806*, edited by Reuben Thwaites in eight volumes; the *History of the*

Expedition under the Command of Lewis and Clark, based on the rewritten Nicholas Biddle edition of 1814 and edited by Elliott Coues in three volumes; and the sworn testimony of Finn Burnett's recollections of Sacagawea. Because the English in Coues' edition is more understandable, all quoted references are from Coues unless otherwise indicated in the text. The quotations from Coues are frequently in the third person, because they were rewritten versions of Lewis's and Clark's journals.

PART I:
The Expedition

1
Jefferson's Dream

WE know little about Sacagawea's early life and childhood. She was probably born in either 1788 or 1789 to Shoshone parents living in the western Rocky Mountains.* While still a small child she had been promised in marriage by her father, who probably received horses or mules in return for her hand. Had events not intervened, she undoubtedly would have followed Shoshone custom and, when she reached the age of thirteen or fourteen, she would have joined the man who was to be her husband. He, in turn, would have then given her father a similar number of horses or mules.

At the age of ten or eleven, Sacagawea traveled eastward with her family and the rest of their band across the Rockies to the area known as Three Forks. There, between what are now the towns of Butte and Bozeman, Montana, three rivers join to form the headwaters of the 2,700 mile long Missouri River.

While Sacagawea's band was camped at Three Forks, it was attacked by a group of gun-bearing Minnetaree (Minnie-tah-ree) warriors on horseback. Sacagawea would later tell Captain Meriwether Lewis how the Shoshone braves, out-numbered and without guns, "mounted their horses and fled as soon as the attack began. The women and children, who had

*A monument now stands near the place where it is thought that she was born—in eastern Idaho, a few miles southeast of the town of Salmon.

been berry-picking, dispersed, and Sacagawea, as she was crossing a shoal place, was overtaken in the middle of the river by her pursuers."

It is not known how long Sacagawea lived as a captive of the Minnetarees. Eventually, however, she became the wife of Toussaint Charbonneau, a French-Canadian interpreter who either bought her or won her from the Minnetaree chief.

Sacagawea could not have known, of course, but at the same time she was beginning her captivity with the Minnetarees, the expedition which would give her name historical significance was being planned. The idea for the exploration of the land between the Mississippi and Columbia Rivers was born in the mind of Thomas Jefferson. A man of restless intelligence, he had always been intensely curious about plants and about animals of the past and present. He felt that it was important to the young United States to know about the unexplored territory—its geography, its fossils and minerals, the life and languages of the Indians living there, and especially about the fur trade, most of which was then conducted and controlled by the British.

Jefferson began laying plans for an expedition as he was about to be inaugurated.[1] As a private citizen, he had made such plans several times, but nothing had come of them. Now as President he felt he would succeed in financing and launching such an expedition. He began by writing to a Virginia friend and neighbor—Meriwether Lewis. Lewis had wanted to join Jefferson's unsuccessful exploration attempt of 1792 but had not been accepted because of his youth.[2] Jefferson knew that Lewis, now in the army, had matured since the earlier attempt. He had become a captain in 1797 and had spent time among the Indians west of Virginia. Jefferson asked the young man to be his private secretary, largely because of his "knowledge of the western country." Lewis, in accepting the position, understood the new President's meaning: "the western exploration scheme again! Disguised, of course."

Jefferson now set about acquiring the money needed to outfit and to man an expeditionary force. Since his last unsuccessful attempt, he had learned all that he could about the area to be explored. Early in 1803, the President wrote a secret message to Congress in which he emphasized the financial advantages of fur trade with the Indians and asked for an appropriation of $2500 "for the purpose of extending the external commerce of the United States," searching out a land route to the Pacific, strengthening American claims to Oregon territory, and gathering information about the Indians and the country of the far west. Congress approved the plan and appropriated the money.

The value of Jefferson's proposed Expedition was greatly enhanced when secret negotiations with France for the purchase of the Louisiana Territory were surprisingly and successfully concluded. Originally, Jefferson had directed his representatives to approach the French with an offer to buy *part* of the Territory, but on October 31, 1803, a treaty was ratified that brought into the United States *all* of the huge area watered by the Missouri River and its tributaries for the bargain price of $16,000,000. In a single stroke, Jefferson had doubled the physical size of the United States and increased the importance of the Expedition which would survey the newly acquired lands.

The President now turned his attention to the details of the Expedition itself. He asked his secretary to choose a companion to share the responsibilities of leadership with him. The first person Lewis thought of was Lieutenant William Clark. The two men had become friends in the 1790s while in the army, dealing with Indians along the Ohio and Mississippi Rivers. "Billy" Clark, Lewis believed, had the knowledge, experience, and personality needed by a leader on a journey through the wilderness. Added to these qualities were his abilities to sketch and make maps for the journals that the President wanted to keep as a record of their observations.

Excited by the letter from Lewis, Clark consulted his brother, General George Rogers Clark, who was eighteen years his senior. The general urged him to accept the invitation and Clark did so,[3] pleasing both Lewis and Jefferson, who had known the Clarks in Virginia before they moved to Kentucky. The choice of Clark proved to be a wise one; during seventeen months of unusually close companionship and of hardships probably beyond imagination today, the leaders disagreed on nothing more important than the taste of dog meat and the necessity of salt in the diet.

Clark's first duty was to recruit men for the Expedition—in Lewis' words: "some good hunters, stout, healthy, unmarried young men, accustomed to the woods and capable of bearing bodily fatigue to a pretty considerable degree." The exploring party would also need carpenters, blacksmiths, and interpreters. At least a hundred young men volunteered to join, but some were weeded out almost at once. Others were found unsuitable during Clark's training of them in the winter of 1803–04. The training camp was across the river from St. Louis, which was to be the starting point of the Expedition up the Missouri.

While on trips making purchases and gathering information Lewis himself found a few men who would join the Expedition. One who was to prove especially valuable was a French-Canadian named Drouillard, whose name was always spelled "Drewyer" by the explorers. Drouillard was an experienced woodsman and hunter. He also knew the Indians well and, because he was an expert in the sign language, he could communicate somewhat with members of any tribe.

Lewis continued preparing himself intellectually for the Expedition. It was to be a scientific exploration, for which Lewis "had a great mass of accurate observation . . . in Zoology, natural history, mineralogy, and astronomy," wrote Jefferson to a friend. Three college professors in Philadelphia, at the President's request, gave Lewis information that would help make him an intelligent observer and reporter of the wild country and of the Indians. The foremost physician of the nation provided medical instruction and advised him about the medicines he should purchase for the trip. A scientist in nearby Lancaster offered advice about the instruments he should take and told him how he should report the latitude and longitude and the climate of the areas he would observe.

The responsibility of purchasing all the supplies fell to Lewis. He supervised the manufacture of firearms for his men, purchased medicines, scientific instruments, tools of many kinds, the framework of a collapsible boat, $2000 worth of gifts for the Indians, twenty barrels of flour and seven barrels of salt. Some of the first matches ever made were given to the Expedition by a French physician. Most of this cargo had to be brought down the Ohio River to the Mississippi.

Early in March 1804, Lewis went from the camp to St. Louis to observe the formal transfer of "the upper Louisiana" from the French flag to the American flag. While there, Lewis obtained all the information he could from the trappers and rivermen he spoke to, some of whom had traveled several hundred miles along the Missouri.

On May 14, 1804, the Lewis and Clark Expedition, also called the Corps of Discovery, began the long struggle of rowing upstream against the stiff current of the Missouri River. There were three boats for the party, which consisted of the two captains, forty-three other men, and Lewis' Newfoundland dog, Scannon, who would bring his master squirrels and wild ducks and whose bark would keep grizzly bears from getting close to camp.

Another possession that proved to be of value to the success of the Expedition was Cruzat's violin. Captain Lewis wrote in his journal on June 25, 1805, "Such as were able to shake a foot amused themselves in dancing on the green to the music of the violin which Cruzatte plays extremely well."

His music gave pleasure not only to the explorers but also to hundreds of Indians who had never before heard a violin. "Our favorite entertainment for the Indians [is] the violin." Again and again, a captain reported that a great many Indians came to see them at their camp. After business matters had been discussed, with the help of Drouillard, Cruzat's violin "was produced and our men danced, to the great delight of the Indians, who remained with us until a late hour."

In the instructions that President Jefferson wrote for Captain Lewis, two of the longest parts are concerned with the Indians. One begins: "In all your dealings with the natives, treat them in the most friendly and conciliatory manner which their conduct will admit. . . ." The President realized that it was impossible for them to foresee how they would be "received by those, whether with hospitality or hostility. . . ." Before the explorers stopped for the winter, they had experienced both.

Captains Lewis and Clark recorded much information about each of the tribes they talked with, some of it amusing. The Indians were fascinated by York, Captain Clark's black servant, the first black person the Indians had ever seen and the first person with kinky hair. They examined him from head to foot; a few even rubbed his skin to see if the color would come off. Pleased with the attention, York told the Indians he was a wild animal, and that Clark had captured and tamed him.

During the last week of October, more and more Indians flocked to the bluffs above the river and to the shore to watch the strangers pass by; some came to their camp in the evenings when, around the fire, the white men square danced with each other to the Indians' great amusement. The Indians who visited the explorers were either Mandans, who lived along the Missouri, or Minnetarees, who lived along the Knife River, which flows from the west into the Missouri. The two tribes were on friendly terms with each other and were used to doing business with white traders.

In a village of a tribe near the Mandans, the Expedition met a French-Canadian, René Jussome, who had lived with Indians for fifteen years and spoke the Mandan language fairly well. Lewis and Clark engaged him as their interpreter, and from him learned a good deal about the people around him. Jussome was married to a Minnetaree woman, and he soon brought her and their children to live with the explorers.

On November 2 Captain Clark found a good wooded site for winter quarters, near what is now Bismarck, North Dakota, in the land of the Mandans. Once they had set up camp, Indian men, women and children flocked to visit, some even staying all night. For a few days, Lewis, Clark, and Drouillard were kept busy by both informal conversations and formal council meetings with the Mandan chiefs and the elders of the villages. Peace was assured by speeches and by ritual smoking of the peace pipe. The captains emphasized the importance of trade for both their people and the Indians. Gifts were received as well as given. The explorers appreciated the bushels of corn brought to them by the Indian women and, later, the half of a buffalo and about 165 pounds of "fine meat" brought to them by the men. Among other gifts, the Mandans received an iron corn mill, which amazed them by the speed with which it ground corn into meal.

In preparation for winter, the explorers began to fell trees for log cabins, but it became so cold by the middle of November that they moved in before the cabins were really completed. During the construction, many Indians came to watch and let their horses graze nearby.

Among the visitors on November 11, wrote Captain Clark in his journal, were two Indian girls who were known among the Minnetarees as the "Snake" (Shoshone) wives of Toussaint Charbonneau, a French-Canadian born in Montreal, and an interpreter for the traders and Indians of the area.* One of the two Shoshone wives is not mentioned again in either Clark's or Lewis's journal. The other was Sacagawea.

*On Christmas Day of 1804, Sergeant Gass and Private Joseph White-house wrote that the only females at their dance were the three wives "to our interpreter, who took no part except the amusement of looking on."

2
Sacagawea Joins the Expedition

IN 1924, the Commissioner of Indian Affairs asked Dr. Charles Eastman, a distinguished Native American,* to research the later life and death of Sacagawea. At Fort Berthold, North Dakota, Eastman interviewed a woman known as Mrs. Weidemann whose father, Chief Poor Wolf, was "about eight or nine" when the Lewis and Clark Expedition spent the winter near his tribe, the Hidatsas, in 1805. His memory of Sacagawea's arrival and involvement with the Expedition comes through his daughter.

While these white men stopped with us that winter, a Frenchman named Charbonneau came down from the north with two Shoshone wives. [There is some evidence that they actually arrived before Lewis and Clark.] He was soon employed by Lewis and Clark. These two Shoshone women were very young, one being about sixteen years old and one about eighteen. . . . This Frenchman had married the two girls somewhere up north. Otter Woman, the older wife, had a son about two years old. He was named for his father, Toussaint Charbonneau. . . .

One fact that Chief Poor Wolf must have forgotten was that the younger wife, Sacagawea, was close to giving birth to her first child.

On February 11, 1805, a few weeks after her first encounter with the white men, Sacagawea went into labor. The baby was slow in coming and Sacagawea suffered much pain.

*See page 110.

Although the journals do not mention the child's father, Charbonneau, they do note that the Frenchman, Jussome, himself an experienced father, suggested that Sacagawea be given small portions of a rattlesnake's rattle. Lewis, who was skeptical about the benefits of Jussome's suggestion, happened to have a rattle with him. Jussome broke two rings of it into small pieces, gave them to Sacagawea, and ten minutes later a fine boy was born. (Despite its success, Lewis noted in his journal that there would have to be further experiments before he would believe in the value of a rattle in childbirth.) The baby was named Jean Baptiste, nicknamed "Pomp" by Lewis, and called simply Baptiste by the Indians he lived with as an adult.

During that winter, the captains had learned that the Indians with horses living nearest to the Rocky Mountains were the Shoshones. Because the explorers needed horses to carry their baggage over the mountains, they needed a Shoshone speaker to purchase the horses for them. Jussome could speak Mandan and Charbonneau Minnetaree and some other Missouri River tribe languages but only Sacagawea could speak Shoshone. So, although it is obvious from their journals that the captains neither respected nor liked him, Lewis and Clark hired Charbonneau as an interpreter, specifying that he should bring Sacagawea along.

About the middle of March, Charbonneau said he was unwilling to go with the Expedition except on certain terms, including not having to follow the captains' orders and being allowed to return whenever he wished. The captains refused to accept his conditions and told him that they could do without his services. A few days later, he apologized and agreed to go and "perform the same duties as the rest of the men."

And so on April 7, 1805, when the exploring party set out from its winter quarters at Fort Mandan, it had three new members: Charbonneau, Sacagawea and the baby, Baptiste, not quite two months old, riding in a cradle board on his mother's back. Chief Poor Wolf recalled that "In the spring when Lewis and Clark started north on their journey by boats, they took Sacagawea and her French husband with them and left Otter Woman with us."

Besides Lewis and Clark, the exploring party consisted of three sergeants, York, Drouillard, and the twenty-two other men. Sixteen men of the original party had already been dismissed and had started back down the river, taking with them boxes filled with a variety of articles for President Jefferson: the skeletons of several animals, some living animals, strange plants, samples of Indian dress, a Mandan bow and arrows, a Mandan ear of corn, and written records.

It was the Missouri River, not the young Indian mother, that served as the Expedition's "principal guide." Sacagawea had seen only a small part of the area explored and not since her childhood. Nowhere in the journals is Sacagawea credited with being the Expedition's guide. In fact, that misconception seems to have been consciously created by Eva Emery Dye for her historical novel, *The Conquest*. Mrs. Dye's development of "that faithful Indian woman with her baby on her back, leading those stalwart mountaineers and explorers through the strange land" from "a few dry bones" is one of the enduring fictions of American history. (That development is discussed in depth in Chapters 10 and 11.)

Though she was not the guide for the Expedition, she was important to them as an interpreter and in other ways. Two days into the journey, Sacagawea collected edible roots hidden by small animals in piles of driftwood. The roots were a welcome addition to meat, the principal part of their diet, and Lewis said they tasted like Jerusalem artichokes.

Lewis and Clark's journal for May 14 describes another way in which Sacagawea helped the Expedition. She was seated in the rear of the sailboat on the Missouri River. At the helm was Charbonneau, who could not swim and was "perhaps the most timid waterman in the world." The boat, carrying valuable supplies and equipment, also held the captains and two other men who could not swim.

The day had been so pleasant that, late in the afternoon, Lewis and Clark left the boat and walked along the shore. Suddenly, a squall of wind keeled the boat over precariously. Charbonneau panicked, forgetting the rudder and paying no attention to Cruzat's directions from the bow. The captains shouted orders but could not be heard from the shore because of the wind and rushing water. At last Cruzat threatened to shoot Charbonneau "if he did not take hold of the rudder and do his duty."

The men eventually brought down the sail and righted the boat which was now filled with water. Much of its cargo—including medicines, books, the captains' journals, instruments, and a large part of the merchandise—had floated out. Two men began to bail, and others, with great difficulty, started rowing toward shore. During this confusion, Sacagawea calmly leaned out of the boat and collected nearly everything that had been washed overboard. A few articles were ruined, chiefly the medicines, but two days later most of what she had rescued had been dried, repacked, and placed in the boat.

Captain Lewis ended his report of the mishap with praise of Sacagawea: "the Indian woman, to whom I ascribe equal fortitude and resolution with any person on board at the time of the accident, caught and preserved most of the light articles which were washed overboard."

A few days later, on May 20, the captains named a branch of the Muscleshell River ("a handsome river, about fifty yards wide") Birdwoman's River for Sacagawea, seemingly in appreciation of her calm action.[4] This is, in fact, the only mention in the journals of the meaning of "Sacagawea." (The little river is now called Crooked Creek.)

The journal entries hold many examples of feats that prove Sacagawea was active and strong. "Clark walked on shore the greater part of the day," wrote Lewis, "accompanied by Charbonneau and the Indian woman." Sacagawea would have had the extra burden of her son riding on her back. She must also have been a keen observer, for when the party found some moccasins where Indians had camped, she examined them carefully and declared that they were different from the moccasins of her people and that they had belonged to people living north of the Missouri.

In early June the Expedition had followed the Missouri to a fork of two streams of about equal width, one coming from the north and the other from the south. Which was the main river and which a tributary? Sacagawea could not guide them even here, for if she had any recollection of the area it was from her days as a frightened, captive girl.

For more than three days, Lewis and a few men explored the north fork. Clark and others went down the south fork for a shorter period of time. The captains came to the same conclusion: the stream coming from the south was the Missouri. Lewis gave the other its present name, Maria's River, in honor of a cousin. (Today the name has no apostrophe.) Although the men left at camp had been spending their time dressing skins for garments, the captains regretted the delay. They felt that it was urgent to cross the Rocky Mountains before the winter snows began.

On June 10, near the mouth of Maria's River, Sacagawea fell ill. That she had become an important member of the Expedition is shown by the fact that *both* captain's journals mention that she was very ill and that Clark bled her. As planned, Lewis and four men left the next day to explore the area around the Great Falls of the Missouri.

Every day during their absence, Clark wrote in his journal about Sacagawea's sickness. Because bleeding was a customary remedy for almost every illness at that time, he bled her twice. On June 12, he wrote that she was "verry *sick* so much so that I moved her into the back part of our covered part of the Perogue which is cool, her own situation being a verry hot one in the bottom of the Perogue exposed to the sun."

But on June 14, he reported that her case was somewhat dangerous. He had her swallow bark, probably containing quinine, and also laid it on her body. Despite his efforts, Sacagawea became worse physically and also fell into depression, refusing on June 15 to take her medicines. At that point, "her husband petition[ed] to return." Finally, Charbonneau, who must have been unconcerned despite his petition, "easily prevailed on her to take medicine." Clark wrote, "if she dies, it will be the fault of her husband as I am now convinced."

When Lewis returned on June 16, he "found the Indian woman extremely ill and much reduced by her indisposition." He was concerned not only, he wrote, "for the poor object herself, then with a young child in her arms, [but also] for the consideration of her being our only dependence for a friendly negotiation with the Snake Indians on whom we depend for horses to assist us in our portage from the Missouri to the Columbia River. . . ." Though not a guide, Sacagawea was proving extremely valuable to the Expedition as a person and member of the party.

Examining Sacagawea, Lewis found that her pulse was weak and very irregular and that her arms and fingers showed signs of nervousness. He gave her "two doses of barks and opium" and had her drink only water similar to that in a spring he knew in Virginia, "strongly impregnated with sulphur" and, perhaps, with iron.

Lewis decided to remain near the spring "in order to make some celestial observations, restore the sick woman," and see that everything was ready for the portage around the Great Falls. He reported that Sacagawea "found great relief from the mineral water." She had improved the next day, but he kept her on medicine and mineral water until she was free from pain and fever, her pulse was regular, and she ate heartily of buffalo meat and a rich soup made from it. Soon she was able to walk on shore a little each day.

Charbonneau, characteristically, let her eat "a considerable quantity of white apples in their raw state, together with a considerable quantity of dried fish," and her pain and fever returned. The Frenchman was sharply rebuked for permitting Sacagawea to disobey Lewis' orders. But the next day she was able to walk on shore again and to fish.

On June 24, Lewis reported that "the Indian woman is now perfectly recovered."

Four days later Sacagawea again showed her mettle. While most of the men were busy with the problems of the portage, Clark kept to the low ground along the river to take notes on that area. With him walked Charbonneau and Sacagawea with Baptiste, his bedding and some of his clothes in the cradleboard.

Shortly after they started, Clark noticed a black cloud threatening rain. He hurried his companions away from the river to a shelter of rocks above a deep and dry gully or ravine where he thought they would be secure from the rain. The first shower was not heavy but the wind was almost terrifying.

Suddenly, "a torrent of rain and hail" fell, more violent than any Clark had ever seen.

Before he got out of the bottom of the ravine, the water was up to his waist. Then a stream of water came plunging down the hill, "tearing everything before it" including large rocks and much mud. Sacagawea just had time to grasp her baby in her arms before the cradle was carried down the swift current.

Putting his gun and shot pouch in his left hand and occasionally pushing Sacagawea before him, Clark scrambled up the rocky hillside using only his right hand. Charbonneau had made some attempt to pull up his wife but fear had immobilized him. Charbonneau, Sacagawea and the baby surely would have fallen and drowned if it had not been for Clark.

Sacagawea finally reached the top of the hill with Baptiste in her arms. His cradle, clothes, and bedding were all gone, as was Clark's compass. Sacagawea was so wet and cold that Clark feared her sickness would return. York, looking frantically for his master, showed up at that time. Clark led the group at a run for the camp.

When Clark reached the top of the hill, he saw at least fifteen feet of water below him. At the camp they found that the men had been knocked down by the wind and bruised by the hail—one stone was seven inches across. A few men were bleeding; some had nearly been killed. The next day a search party found the vital compass almost buried by mud. The ravine was full of rocks so large that they would surely have killed Clark and his companions.

The journey around the falls and rapids took one month of preparation and difficult travel, often against a stiff current. Then, on July 22, Sacagawea gave the men cheer by recognizing the country they were passing through. They were not far, she said, from where three rivers come together and where her relatives lived part of the year. The men were thrilled that they would soon see "the head of the Missouri yet unknown to the civilized world."

When they reached the forks, Sacagawea told the story of her capture by the Minnetarees at that spot. Lewis wrote that she showed "no sorrow in recollecting the event or of joy in being again restored to her native country; if she had enough to eat and a few trinkets to wear I believe she would be content anywhere." Her wanderings after the Expedition bear out this statement.

At the Three Forks, the captains gave the rivers the names they retain today. The one coming from the southeast is called the Gallatin, in honor of the Secretary of the Treasury; the south fork, the Madison, for the Secretary of State; the southwest branch, they called the Jefferson River.

Which one would take them to the Rocky Mountains? Here again Sacagawea was not the Expedition's "principal guide"; in fact, the explorers' journals do not even record any suggestion made by her.

The decision was made as it had been at the fork of Marias River. Captain Clark and a few others traveled far enough up the Gallatin and Madison Rivers to know that neither of them would lead to the Rockies. So, after two days of much needed rest, the Expedition started up the Jefferson River, heading west.

3

*S*acagawea on the Jefferson River

CAPTAIN Lewis, Sacagawea, Charbonneau, and two men who were unwell walked along the shore when the explorers started up the Jefferson River on July 30. At Three Forks, Clark had been ill, and Lewis had "made all the celestial observations necessary to fix the longitude of a spot that seems an essential point in the geography of the western world."

Travel continued difficult, whether the river flowed through prairies or between perpendicular cliffs. The current was so strong, the wind from the northwest so severe, the islands so numerous, and the rapids so hazardous (some of them "with a fall of six feet") that it required "the utmost exertions of the men to make any advance." Some of them pushed the boats with poles. Others, on the shore, "drew them by cords."

Sacagawea brightened their spirits on August 8 when she recognized, at a little distance, the tall rock that is still called Beaverhead Rock because its appearance is said to resemble the head of a beaver. (It is in western Montana, between Three Forks and Dillon.) Sacagawea told the captains that the rock is not far from where her people spent the summer "on a river beyond the mountains running toward the west." She felt sure that they were "either on this river [the Jefferson] or on that immediately west of its source."

Captain Lewis saw his duty at once: "As it is now all important with us to meet with these people as soon as possible, I determined to proceed tomorrow with a small party to the principal stream of this river and pass the mountains to the Columbia and down that river until I found the Indians; in short, it is my resolution to find them or some others with horses, if it should cause me a trip of one month. . . without horses, we shall be obliged to leave a great part of our stores, of which it appears to me that we have already a stock sufficiently small for the length of the voyage before us."

Between August 8 and August 17, Sacagawea is mentioned in the journals only three times. One evening at dinner, Charbonneau struck his wife, and Captain Clark "gave him a severe reprimand." On August 15, she and Captain Clark narrowly escaped being bitten by rattlesnakes.

On August 16, Private Joseph Whitehouse wrote in his journal that Captain Clark, the interpreter, and his wife, walking along the shore, found a great number of the fruit called serviceberries. Sacagawea gathered a pail full of them and gave them to the explorers at noon when they stopped in a grove of cottonwood trees.

When Captain Lewis referred to Sacagawea (not by name), he was west of the Continental Divide in the camp of the Shoshones beside a river flowing west. Sacagawea's recognition of Beaverhead Rock (the last familiar spot she saw on the way to the Pacific) had assured the captains that by following the Jefferson River they would find her people.

The boats would continue to creep and crawl through the shallow water and around the many curves. Captain Lewis would continue what he had been doing the first six days of August—traveling on foot to look for the Shoshones.

After breakfast on August 9, Lewis, Droulliard (the expert with the sign language), Shields, and McNeal flung their knapsacks over their backs and started westward on foot. Captain Lewis was determined to find Indians with horses, no matter how long they were separated from the party.

Not since the explorers left the Mandans had they seen a single Indian! A few footprints along a shore, a pair of

moccasins that Sacagawea said did not belong to her people,
smoke signals at a distance—these were the only evidences of
Indians that the Expedition had seen for four months.

On the second morning, Lewis and his three companions
came to an old Indian road and saw on it the prints of horses'
hooves. They followed it over hills, occasionally along the
narrow river bottom, until they reached a place where the
Jefferson divides into two nearly equal branches.

They explored both creeks. Finding that the forks were "at
the westernmost point of the Jefferson River," Lewis wrote a
note to Clark advising him to stay there with the main party
until he and his men returned. He fastened the note to a dry
willow pole at the forks of the river—a dry pole, so that a
beaver would not eat it, as one had done with an earlier note.

Two days after starting, Captain Lewis saw "with the
greatest delight, an Indian man on horseback, at the distance
of two miles, coming down the plain toward them." Carefully
he moved toward the man, determined not to frighten him. A
mile from them, the Indian suddenly stopped. Lewis stopped
also. He took his blanket from his knapsack and with it made
"the universal sign of friendship among the Indians" of the
region. Three times he made this sign of friendship but the Indian did not move. With suspicion, he watched Droulliard
and Shields approach him from different directions. Lewis
knew that his men would not hear him and that a signal
would add to the Indian's alarm. He put down his gun,
moved slowly, and did everything he could think of to assure
the man of his peaceful intentions. But when Lewis came
close to him, the Indian suddenly turned his horse, leaped
across the creek, and disappeared among the willow bushes.

The next day, as they trudged up the mountain, the stream
gradually became smaller. After two miles, McNeal, "in a fit
of enthusiasm [stood] with one foot on each side of the river"
and said, joyfully, "I thank God that I have lived to bestride
the Missouri."

Four miles later, after an abrupt turn in the river westward,
"they reached a small gap formed by the high mountains,
which recede on each side, leaving room for the Indian road."
(This gap is now known as Lemhi Pass.) The men followed

that road through hills and soon reached "the top of a ridge,
from which they saw high mountains, partially covered with
snow, still to the west of them. The ridge . . . formed the
dividing line between the waters of the Atlantic and Pacific
oceans."

They were standing on the Continental Divide!

Going down a steep slope, they soon "reached a handsome,
bold creek of cold, clear water, running to the westward.
They stopped to taste for the first time the waters of the
Columbia. [Soon] they reached a spring on the side of a
mountain, [near] some dry willow brush for fuel." There they
camped for the night.

The following morning, after walking through a valley for
a few miles, they happened upon two women and a little girl.
The younger woman immediately fled in fright, but the
elderly woman and the little girl were so terrified that they
held their heads down as if waiting to be killed. Lewis calmed
them by giving them gifts and by painting their cheeks a
bright red. He had learned from Sacagawea that the little
ceremony of painting cheeks was a sign of peace among the
Shoshones. Through Droulliard, he persuaded the woman to
recall her companion. Lewis gave beads and trinkets to her
also and painted her cheeks with red paint. The women were
then easily persuaded to lead the strangers to their camp.
Almost immediately they were faced by about sixty warriors,
riding on excellent horses at top speed, led by their chief and
two sub-chiefs. Lewis put down his gun and walked ahead,
carrying his flag. The women showed their gifts and talked
with the chief.

He and his sub-chiefs "immediately leaped from their
horses, came up to Lewis and embraced him with great
cordiality." All the other warriors followed their chief's action. Lewis, of course, was delighted by the peaceful reactions, but wrote later "we were all so caressed and besmeared
with their greasepaint that I was heartily tired of their
national hug."

The chief sent four young men ahead to their camp to
make preparations for a council. But formal ceremony began
where they were—seated in a circle around the four white

men. Lewis lighted his pipe and offered it to the chief, but
another ceremony had to precede the smoking of the peace
pipe. Every Indian pulled off his moccasins—a custom, Lewis
learned, "which indicates the sacred sincerity of their profes-
sions when they smoke with a stranger." Removing the
moccasins meant that a person would go barefooted the rest
of his life if he were not faithful to his promises. After a little
formal smoking, the men put on their moccasins, and all
started forth to the Shoshone camp on the bank of a river.

There all went into a leathern lodge which the four young
men had prepared for the council. Seated on green boughs
and antelope skins around a central fire, the Indians again
took off their moccasins. This time, the chief asked Lewis and
his men to remove theirs. An elaborate pipe-smoking ceremony followed, in which was used the chief's pipe of trans-
parent green stone that had been very highly polished.

Captain Lewis, through Droulliard, explained the purposes
of his visit. "By this time all the women and children in the
camp had gathered round the lodge," to see the first white
men they had ever heard of. Lewis gave them the rest of his
small gifts.

Lewis and Droulliard spent considerable time with Chief
Cam-ē-àh-wait. The captain did not hurry, for he knew that it
would take Clark and his men several days to reach the note
left for him. He also found it difficult to persuade Chief
Cameahwait to meet the other white chief and his larger body
of men. They would be waiting at the forks of the river, Lewis
said, ready to trade with the Shoshones. But the Indians were
suspicious that the strangers might be in league with an
enemy tribal ambush.

In these meetings with the chief, Lewis recorded much
information about the Shoshones. One of the principal purposes of the exploration, in President Jefferson's mind, was to
gather information about the Indians of the Northwest. Some
anthropologists of recent years have learned from Captain
Lewis's journal the earliest known facts about the Indian
tribes that he visited.

Helpful though Droulliard was with the sign language,
Captain Lewis told Chief Cameahwait, several times, that with

the main party was a Shoshone woman who had been taken prisoner by the Minnetarees. With her as an interpreter, he felt that he could explain himself more fully than he could with signs.

At last he was successful. The chief and eight warriors started with the explorers about noon on August 15. Gradually, others joined them. In a short time, "all of the men of the nation and a number of the women had overtaken them, having changed from the surly ill-temper in which they were two hours ago, to the greatest cheerfulness and gayety." Some of them had been persuaded to go by learning that with the white men was a man who was black all over and had short, kinky hair.

Early the next evening, they came in sight of the forks, about two miles away. But they saw no people, no boats. The Indians' fears returned. To calm them, Lewis handed his gun to the chief, and his men handed theirs to three warriors. Captain Lewis pretended a cheerfulness he did not feel. As he would later write, "I slept little as might be expected, my mind dwelling on the state of the Expedition which I have ever held in equal estimation with my own existence. . . .I had mentioned to the chief several times that we had with us a woman of his nation who had been taken prisoner by the Minnetarees, and that by means of her I hoped to explain myself more fully than I could with signs." Chief Cameahwait and five warriors lay beside him. The rest of the Indians hid themselves in the willow-brush.

The next morning all worries vanished. A Shoshone who had wandered alone a short distance down the river came rushing back with good news: he had seen men dragging boats in the water! The Indians "all seemed transported with joy," reported Lewis, "and the chief repeated his fraternal hug. I felt quite as much gratified by this information as the Indians appeared to be."

On August 17, Captain Clark, Charbonneau, and Sacagawea left the boats at seven o'clock in the morning and walked along the shore. Clark was about one hundred yards behind "the interpreter and interpretess" when, after about a mile,

Sacagawea "began to dance and to show every mark of the most extravagant joy." Now and then, she turned around toward him and pointed to several Indians whom he saw advancing. At the same time, she sucked her fingers, to indicate that they were her own people. Among them was Drouillard, dressed like a Shoshone Indian.

As the three approached the camp of the Indians who had come over the mountains with the white men, a young woman ran from the crowd, with arms outstretched. She and Sacagawea "embraced with the most tender affection."

"The meeting of these two young women had in it something peculiarly touching, not only from the ardent manner in which their feelings were expressed, but also from the real interest of their situation. They had been companions in childhood, in the war with the Minnetarees they had both been taken prisoners in the same battle; they had shared and softened the rigors of their captivity till one of them had escaped from the Minnetarees, with scarce a hope of ever meeting her friend relieved from the hands of her enemies."

While Sacagawea was visiting with friends of her childhood, Captain Clark was welcomed by Captain Lewis and by Chief Cameahwait. The Chief, "after the first embraces and salutations were over, conducted him to a sort of circular tent or shade of willows." Other Shoshone men were with them for a council. The Chief first seated Clark on a white robe and tied six white shells like pearls in his red hair. Both the Shoshones and the white men removed their moccasins, as a sign of peace and, after much ceremony, the peace pipe was passed around for each man to smoke.

When the time came for the conference, Sacagawea was sent for. She came into the shaded circle, sat down, and was about to interpret when she looked across at the Chief. Instantly, she jumped up, ran across the little circle, embraced him, threw her blanket over their heads, and burst into tears.

Chief Cameahwait was her brother!

"The chief himself was moved, but not in the same degree." After brief conversation, Sacagawea returned to her seat and tried to interpret, but her tears frequently interrupted.

Finn Burnett, a frontiersman, many years later said: "Finally, when they had managed to contact these Indians [the Shoshones], Sacagawea was overjoyed to discover her brother, Chief Cameahwait, among them. After a joyful reunion, she began to talk the language of her childhood again, and told him that the white men wished to cross the mountains. She explained that Lewis and Clark needed Shoshones for guides, and a sufficient number of ponies to transport their provisions and equipment to the headwaters of the Columbia River" (Robert David, *Finn Burnett: Frontiersman*). (Additional recollections of Finn Burnett are given in Chapter 15.)

When the council ended, she learned that all her family were dead except the Chief, another brother (not then with his people), and the young son of her oldest sister. Sacagawea immediately adopted the small boy. According to Shoshone custom, she would consider him her son and he would consider her his mother. Naturally, she left him with his uncles. He was not mentioned in the journals again.

In a short time, the remainder of the exploring party arrived with the canoes. Their journey had been slow because the stream was so shallow that the men had to wade through the icy water and drag the boats against the rapids. The crookedness of the stream added to their difficulties, so that some of the men were almost exhausted.

In a meadow near the forks of the river, the men used sails and willow poles to make a shady spot for the council in the late afternoon. Through interpreters, Captain Lewis began to explain to Chief Cameahwait, his sub-chiefs, and their warriors the purposes of the white men's visit.

He emphasized the friendly attitude of his government, the advantages of trade between the two nations, and their desire to find the best route to the land beyond the mountains. Their immediate need, he said, was about thirty horses to carry their baggage across to the Shoshone village. There, they would purchase as many horses as could be spared. They would also need a guide to show them the best route through and over the mountains.

Chief Cameahwait was favorably impressed by Captain Lewis's speech. He replied that they did not have enough horses with them at the time, but promised that on the next day he would return to his village, bring all of his own horses to the white men, and try to persuade his men to come back with theirs.

The council was a long one, partly because everything had to be said in four languages: English, French, Minnetaree, and Shoshone. Not only Sacagawea and Charbonneau were with the captains, but also Labiche. At the beginning of the journey, Labiche and Cruzat were listed as "two French watermen." At the end, Labiche was said to have given "very essential services as a French and English interpreter, and sometimes as an Indian interpreter."

The captains felt satisfied with the conference. Their several gifts to Chief Cameahwait, two other chiefs, and two promising young warriors included a small medal for each. The one given to Cameahwait had the likeness of President Jefferson on one side, and, on the other, a "figure of hands clasped with a pipe and a tomahawk." Apparently, one of these Jefferson medals was also given to Sacagawea in honor of her services. The medal given to each of the others bore the likeness of General Washington. The white men also gave the Indians an antelope that one of their hunters had brought in.

That evening Lewis and Clark made their plans for the next few days. The Shoshones had given them alarming descriptions of the river that flows westward from their area to the big river flowing farther westward—the Columbia. So it was decided that Clark and eleven men should start the next morning to discover whether it was practical to go down the river now called the Salmon (in Idaho). They would take with them not only their arms but also their tools for making canoes, if the river was navigable and if there was timber.

The next morning, the captains purchased three horses from the Shoshones to relieve the small exploring party of the heavy weight of the necessary equipment. The Indians seemed quite as well pleased with the bargain as the captains did.

Before noon on August 18, all the Indians except two men and two women started out in good humor. Captain Clark and eleven others of the exploring party would accompany them to the Shoshone camp west of the Continental Divide. Chief Cameahwait and others could certainly be the guides through the Lemhi Pass. Sacagawea, her baby, and her husband went with them. Clark would leave Sacagawea and Charbonneau at the Shoshone camp with the hope that they would hasten the departure of several Indians with their horses. Lewis and the remainder of the party would prepare the baggage for transportation over the mountains. They would wait for Chief Cameahwait and his horses at the camp near the fork of the Jefferson River on the east side of the Rockies.

A rainy evening followed the departure of Clark, Sacagawea, Charbonneau, and the others. August 18, 1805, was Lewis's thirty-first birthday. While writing his journal, he took time for an unusually personal entry. He surmised that he had lived about half of his life "and had as yet done but little, very little indeed, to further the happiness of the human race or to advance the information of the succeeding generation. . . .

"I dash from the gloomy thought, and resolve in future to redouble my exertions and at least endeavor to promote those two primary objects of human existence, by giving them the aid of that portion of talents which nature and fortune have bestowed upon me; or in [the] future to live *for mankind,* as I have heretofore lived *for myself.*"

4

Journey over the Rockies

TWO days after Captain Clark and his men had left the camp east of the mountains, they and a Shoshone guide started toward the Salmon River. The next day Chief Cameahwait, Sacagawea, Charbonneau, and about fifty men, with their women and children, started eastward across the mountains to the explorers' camp.

There, while the horses grazed, Lewis held a council. Through his interpreters, he addressed the chiefs and warriors after the usual giving of gifts to the chiefs. Then "all the Indians were treated with an abundant meal of boiled Indian corn and beans. The poor wretches... had been almost starved, and received this new luxury with great thankfulness."

Lewis gave Cameahwait a few dried squashes that had been brought from the Mandans. They were boiled, and the taste delighted the chief. In fact, he said that it was the best food he had ever eaten, except for the lump of sugar his sister had given him. He would be happy, he said, to live where such good things were produced. Lewis assured him that it would not be long before the white men would make it possible for him and his people "to live below the mountains, where they might cultivate all these kinds of food, instead of wandering in the mountains."

In this frame of mind, the Shoshones were soon persuaded to sell "five very good horses on very reasonable terms." Toward evening the explorers "caught 528 very good fish, most of them large trout," and gave nearly all of them to the Indians. Lewis was eager to start westward, but Chief Cameahwait persuaded him to wait until another party of Shoshones arrived.

While two white men and several Indians went hunting for much-needed game, Lewis had his men sink the canoes in the river and fill them with stones. They would be safe there, he thought, both from floods and fire. They had already made pack saddles and had secretly hidden everything that could not be taken across the mountains. They hoped that the canoes and the buried articles could be quickly made ready for use on the way back from the Pacific.

In the middle of the afternoon of August 23, the expected party of Shoshones arrived, about fifty men, women, and children. Through his interpreters, Lewis learned that they were on their way down the valley to the buffalo country. He felt some fear that Cameahwait and his men might go with this party, but they continued to say that they would accompany the white men.

About noon on August 24, the explorers and the Indians started westward. Horses and mules that had been purchased or borrowed carried most of the baggage. The rest was placed on the shoulders of women. All members of the Expedition, except Sacagawea, started on foot. With articles given him by Captain Lewis, Charbonneau had purchased a horse for her to ride. One of the Indians politely offered Lewis a horse for the journey, so that he could better direct the party.

They started at sunrise and stopped for dinner at noon. They were about two miles east of Lemhi Pass, which Lewis had already crossed twice and Clark had crossed on August 19. At dinner, Lewis had reason to be disappointed in Chief Cameahwait, disgusted with Charbonneau, and grateful to Sacagawea for her loyalty to the Expedition.

Chief Cameahwait had impressed both captains as being sincere and friendly. But Sacagawea had told Charbonneau early in the morning that her brother had sent messengers ahead to ask the remainder of his people to break camp and to join him the next day for a hunting trip in the buffalo country. Charbonneau was "seemingly unconcerned." Not until several hours had passed and after seventeen miles of travel by foot did he give Sacagawea's message to the captain.

Lewis was alarmed by the information that he would soon be stranded without enough horses to go farther. He was so "out of patience" with Charbonneau's stupidity and delay that he spoke to the interpreter sharply. He held a meeting with Cameahwait and his two sub-chiefs. He reminded them of their promise and appealed to their sense of honor, as well as to their need for future trade with the white people. The two sub-chiefs quickly replied that they had wanted to keep their word and to assist the white men. They said that the first chief was solely responsible for the change of plans. Cameahwait was silent for some time. Then, admitting that he had done wrong, he explained: "I was so conscious of the hunger of my people that I wished to hasten the buffalo hunt." He immediately sent one of his men ahead to tell their people to remain at home until the chiefs returned.

When white hunters joined the party that evening, they had only one deer. "As a proof of his sincerity, Lewis gave it to the women and children and remained supperless himself."

Late the next afternoon, they reached the Shoshone camp in a beautiful meadow along what is now called the Lemhi River. It was about three miles farther up the river than the one Lewis and his three companions had visited. The leathern lodge was in the center of thirty-two brush or grass huts. There they found Colter, one of the men who had gone with Captain Clark, and the old Shoshone guide, whom the white men called Old Toby.

Colter gave Captain Lewis a note from Captain Clark, who reported "that there were no hopes of a passage by water, and that the most practicable route seemed to be that mentioned by his guide, toward the north."

That meant more horses, more information about the best route to take—and more need for the interpreters. Lewis told Cameahwait that they would like to purchase twenty more horses. The chief replied that a large number of their horses had been stolen the previous spring, but he hoped that he could spare twenty.

"To keep the Indians as cheerful as possible," Cruzat played his violin that evening and the men danced, to the great enjoyment of their observers.

Two mornings later, Captain Clark and his men returned from their exploration of the Salmon River. The purchase of horses continued, but the captains were unable to obtain a horse for each man. The hunters did secure enough deer for three days in succession, and their diet of parched corn was over for a short time.

On August 30, the Expedition said farewell to the Shoshones as the Indians started toward the buffalo country east of the Rockies. At the same time, the explorers started northward on a road beside the Lemhi River, which flows down to the Salmon River; all their baggage was carried by horses. Old Toby, a Shoshone, and his four sons, and another Indian became guides for the Expedition. On September 2, all the Indians departed except Old Toby and one of his sons—and of course Sacagawea. Carrying her baby on her back, she rode on the horse that Captain Lewis had provided for her. Old Toby, then, was the first actual guide of the Expedition.

At first they traveled along the fairly plain road that Captain Clark and his party had followed when they went to explore the Salmon River. In the valleys they saw several fires that were signals to the bands of Shoshones and Flatheads to gather for the trip to the Buffalo country. But soon they were cutting their way through "thickets of trees and brush," climbing through a dense evergreen forest, and pushing their way up steep and rocky slopes. Their horses sometimes slipped and were injured by the sharp rocks. One day the hunters were kept too busy to hunt, and so everyone "passed an uncomfortable night." The next day they climbed a seemingly verticle slope to cross a mountain "at 7,000 feet or more."

Men and horses became very fatigued. And the weather turned bad: rain was followed by snow and then later by sleet. On the morning of September 4, they found the ground covered with two inches of snow and they were forced to wait until the ice on their baggage had melted.

In the late afternoon, they saw a large camp of Indians in the valley before them. When they reached the camp and alighted from their horses, they "were received with great cordiality." The Indians spread white robes over the captains' shoulders and smoked the pipe of peace with the party. This was a band of Salish Indians (now usually called the Flatheads, although it was never a tribal custom to flatten their heads). This group of about 80 men and 300 women and children (and "at least 500 horses") were on their way to meet other bands at Three Forks.

The Indians were so cordial and kind that the explorers camped beside them for two nights and almost two days. The first morning, they started to hold a council. Through interpreters, the captains explained the purposes of their journey. "But we could not talk with them as much as we wish," wrote Private Joseph Whitehouse in his journal, "for all that we say has to go through six languages before it gets to them." Lewis and Clark soon turned to the easier and "more intelligible language of gifts."

Chief Three Eagles gave the white chiefs some otter fur and the skins of two antelopes; the women gave them dried roots and berries. The captains exchanged seven of their horses and bought thirteen others. In spite of the difficulties of language, Lewis reported, as usual, information about these people for President Jefferson, and "procured a vocabulary of their language."

In the afternoon of September 6, both groups left the camp. According to Salish tradition, the explorers were directed to "the best way to get to the Nez Perce country on the west side of the mountains."

In the summer of 1953, one of the authors of this book (E.E.C.) recorded the Salish tradition of the coming of the Lewis and Clark Expedition, from an elderly man and woman on the Flathead Reservation in western Montana. The man, Pierre Pichette, blind since he was fourteen, had been trained by his elders to be tribal historian. (He was the last historian of that tribe, and he died the following winter.) The explorers were "a puzzling sight to all the Indians surrounding them," Pichette said. They were puzzled also by the man who had painted himself with charcoal! Shortly before the strangers left, Pichette recollected, Chief Three Eagles said to his people, "This party is the first of this kind of people we have ever seen. They have been brought in safely. I want them taken out safely. I want you warriors to go with them part of the way to make sure that they leave our country without harm." Through an interpreter, the ninety-year-old woman, whose Indian name means "Painted-Hem-of-the-Skirt," told essentially the same story in 1953. She ended her account of the coming of the Lewis and Clark Expedition [in 1805] with these words: "Chief Three Eagles told his people that they must not harm the strangers in any way. No one has ever heard of the Salish people and the whites getting into battle. . . . They would have fought their own Indian friends to keep them from harming the white people."

Soon after leaving the Salish camp, the explorers were traveling northward along the Bitterroot River. On September 9, 1805, they stopped for two nights along what they named Travelers' Rest Creek (now called Lolo Creek). They had used all of their flour and most of their corn and berries, and Old Toby told them that they would find little game for some distance. While the hunters attempted to add to the food supply, other men repaired their clothes. Very likely Sacagawea had some mending and laundry to do.

On September 16, the explorers rode over snow-covered rocks and through falling snow. More snow dropping from the trees kept them "continually wet to the skin" and very cold. Clark and one man went ahead to have the fires ready for the others. Unable to find game or fish, they twice had to kill colts. Once they had to melt snow for drinking water.

On September 18, they reached the northernmost part of this journey. In fourteen days they had traveled north from a little south of present-day Salmon, Idaho to a little south of present-day Missoula, Montana. By paved highway today, it would take about three hours.

The hardships of the journey north over the Rockies were but a preparation for those that had to be endured on the journey westward. Again and again, the Expedition had to climb steep and rocky slopes to cross a mountaintop 5,000 to 7,000 feet high. Again the horses slipped; one of them rolled over and over for about forty yards until stopped by a tree, "but the poor animal escaped without much injury." Two horses became so exhausted they had to be left behind.

The following June, when they were preparing for their return over the Rockies, Clark wrote these words about their first experiences: "not any of us have yet forgotten our sufferings in these mountains in September last. I think it probable we never shall."

The spirits of the men became seriously low because of their fatigue, the lack of food, and their dreary prospects. So early in the morning of September 18, Clark and six hunters started forth, hoping to find game that they could send back to the main party. To the first creek that Captain Clark's party camped beside, they gave the appropriate name of Hungry Creek. Next morning, without breakfast—following an evening without supper—they rode for six miles over a road more steep and stony than any they had yet traveled. Fortunately, they found a stray horse. They breakfasted on it and then hung the remainder on a tree for the main party. Lewis and his companions found it the next day, to "the great joy" of the men—but not of Sacagawea. The thought of eating dogs and horses was abhorrent to her, as it was to the Shoshones in general.

5

Down Three Rivers to the Pacific

ON the same day, September 20, Captain Clark and his hunters descended the most westward of the Rocky Mountains. When they came out of the deep forest, a beautiful prairie lay before them. It is now known as Weippe Prairie, in eastern Idaho across the state from Lewiston.

Five miles farther, three Indian boys were playing. Frightened by the strangers, they ran off and hid in the deep grass. Clark dismounted, gave his reins and his gun to his men, and walked over to the boys. Soon they lost their fear and started off to their camp with ribbons as gifts.

In a short time an Indian man met the explorers and led them to a large tepee in the camp. All the people gathered round "to view with a mixture of fear and pleasure these wonderful strangers." With signs, the white men were told that this tepee was the residence of the great chief and that he and his warriors would be away for two weeks or more.

Soon the Indians placed before the strangers "a small piece of buffalo meat, some dried salmon, berries, and several kinds of roots. . . . After the long abstinence," wrote Clark, "this was a sumptuous treat." The roots, which he praised highly, were bulbs called camas, very important to the Indians of a wide area. The captain gave the Indians a few gifts, and then the white men were led by a sub-sub-chief to a camp two miles farther along the prairie. On their way, they saw women digging roots. At the second camp the white men also "were treated with great kindness," and spent the night there.

That evening and all the next day, Clark was sick, probably from eating such hearty food after his long fast. He sent the hunters for game and busied himself with gathering information about the people and about the best route to Big River. (In several languages of the Pacific Northwest Indians, the name of the Columbia means "Big River.") When the hunters returned and reported that they had had no luck, Clark bought all the food from the Indians that he could, in exchange for articles he had with him. One of his men and an Indian hired by the captain started with the food to Captain Lewis and the main party.

That afternoon, guided by an Indian, Clark and his men rode down to the river now called the Clearwater to talk with Chief Twisted Hair. He was the second chief of his band, then fishing near the forks of the river. The next morning Clark sent his hunters to try their luck again. Accompanied by Chief Twisted Hair and his son, Captain Clark rode back up the hill and across most of the level plain. Shortly after sunset, the three reached the camp near the forest and there found that Captain Lewis and the main party had just arrived. Lewis told Clark that on the afternoon when the two men with food reached them, "they had tasted nothing since the night before."

When the Expedition reached the Chō'-pun-nish in September 1805, no one could have foreseen that they would spend considerable time with these people, both then and the following spring. For generations, white people have called them the Nez Perce Indians, because the first French traders gave them this name, which means "pierced nose."

These Indians, whom the Expedition were to be with for the next two weeks, lived in two villages consisting "of about thirty double tents," wrote Clark in his journal. Lewis, the following day, described in considerable detail their dress and their many ornaments of beads and shells. He included a brief statement about "a single shell of wampum through the nose."

"We question this statement," say the Nez Perces in their recent book *Noon Nee-Me-Poo* (*We, the Nez Perces*). "They were talking about some other tribe." And Kate McBeth, who was a missionary among them for many years, beginning in 1879, wrote: "The Nez Perces deny that they ever did, as a tribe, pierce the nose. Occasionally one did." But very recently, archaeologists digging in the Nez Perce area have found many skeletons, each with a shell in the nose. "Anthropologists suppose that the old custom had disappeared soon after Lewis and Clark reported what they saw."

The coming of the Lewis and Clark Expedition to the Nez Perces was a favorite story around the winter fires for generations. In the early 1950s, three elderly Nez Perces were interviewed, and each related the tradition heard many times in their youth and which they had told many times when they were grandparents. One old woman, telling her story through an interpreter, began with laughter: her ancestors had been afraid of the strangers because of the hair on their faces! Another grandmother, a graduate of Carlisle School for Indians, spoke excellent English, and after a morning of storytelling, she played delightful waltzes on her piano. Both women told about Watkuese and Lewis and Clark. *Wat-ku-ese* means "Escaped and Returned to Her Own Country." She, like Sacagawea, had been captured by an enemy tribe, but returned to her own people. While traveling alone, hundreds of miles, Watkuese had been very kindly treated by all the white people she met. Because the white people had befriended her, the Nez Perces welcomed Lewis and Clark, according to their oral tradition.

The Nez Perce men gave the captains a good deal of information that proved helpful during the rest of their journey to the ocean. On white elk skin, Chief Twisted Hair drew a map of the three rivers they would travel down—a journey of about twelve days, he said. Others gave them the same information. (On today's maps the Clearwater River flows into the Snake River at Lewiston, Idaho, and Clarkston, Washington. The Snake River flows into the Columbia River at Pasco, in south-central Washington. The Columbia, during the rest of its 1,200 mile journey from the Rocky Mountains of Canada to the Pacific, forms the boundary between the states of Washington and Oregon.)

The captains, as usual, explained the purposes of their Expedition and gave the Nez Perces gifts. Then they purchased as much food as the horses in their weakened condition could carry down to the Clearwater River. As usual, great crowds of Indians stayed around the explorers all night. In the morning of September 23, they passed many women digging and dressing camas roots for winter use, and great piles of bulbs heaped on the plain. Weippe Prairie was (and still is) a favorite camas roots area for the Indians of the region.

When the Expedition started that morning, Captain Lewis could hardly sit on his horse since he (and several others) had been sick the evening before. Some men had to be helped to their saddles; others had to lie beside the road before they could ride farther. When they reached the Nez Perce camp beside the river, they learned that two of the hunters were ill and that the group had brought back only two deer.

Nearly everyone was sick the next day. The weather was oppressively hot after the coolness of the mountains. The diet of roots produced violent pains in the stomachs of some men. So on October 2, they killed a horse for soup as well as meat. The captains had already decided that it would be wiser to build canoes and float down the rivers than to ride farther.

As the men became able, they felled trees and built five canoes—four large ones and a small one for scouting ahead.[5] Captain Lewis, who had never fully recovered, became ill a second time, and so did Captain Clark. But somehow, on October 7, the canoes were completed, the baggage packed in them, the saddles buried, and the thirty-eight horses branded and marked. Three Nez Perces promised to take good care of the horses until the white men returned.

The Expedition started down the Clearwater River, with three young Nez Perces who remained with them until they reached the junction of the Snake River and the Columbia. One of them guided the party. On October 8, they were joined by two Nez Perce chiefs, who proved helpful in making friends for the explorers. Sometimes the chiefs walked ahead for that purpose; they were also helpful with interpreting. They remained with the Expedition until October 25, then started home by horse.

It was salmon fishing time. Consequently, many Indians were camped near the ripples and the rapids, on the shore and on the many islands bordered with rocks.

The members of the Expedition rejoiced that the journey down the three rivers would mean no rowing against a stiff current, no poling and dragging boats in shallow water. They could not foresee the new hardships of the journey downstream. During the first hours of travel, they passed ten rapids. One canoe hit a rock that caused a leak. A rock made a hole in the side of another canoe, and it immediately filled with water and sank. Men who could not swim clung to its sides, while their companions in another boat rowed to the shore, unloaded it, and rowed back to rescue them. The Expedition was delayed an entire day for the repair of the canoe and the drying of the supplies.

From their first day's experience, the white men had learned from the Nez Perce guide to explore ahead any dangerous looking ripples strewn with many rocks. They learned also to have the small canoe go ahead, piloted by the Nez Perce guide, followed by the others.

The captains were surprised to learn that Old Toby and one of his sons, their Shoshone guides, had been seen running upstream several miles behind them. They had made no explanation to anyone about their departure on October 7 and had received no pay for their work of 38 days. Apparently they had had enough travel by water, through rapids and around huge rocks. Obviously, they were no longer needed as guides.

When the explorers reached the Snake River, Indians flocked from all directions to see the white men. In recent years, great-grandparents have told interesting stories about being taken when they were tiny children to see strangers with hair on their faces.

Needing some food besides salmon and roots, the captains decided to buy a few dogs. "They felt no distaste for this new dish" because they had become used to horse flesh. The men gained weight and looked healthier than they had for weeks. The captains purchased forty dogs later when they were ready to leave their camp near the junction of the Snake and the Columbia rivers.

Thanks again to the Nez Perce chiefs' having gone ahead, the Expedition had been given a very hearty welcome at the junction, an important spot. Just as the explorers finished making camp, they heard the beating of drums accompanied by singing. A chief and a procession of about 200 men were marching south from their camp along the Columbia. Soon they formed a semicircle around the strangers and continued singing for some time.

The explorers spent most of three days, October 16 to 18, with these people who were related to the Nez Perces by language. The captains needed time to obtain and record the various kinds of information that had been requested by President Jefferson. More than a century later, on October 16, 1927, the area where the Expedition camped was dedicated as Sacagawea State Park, a popular recreation area near present-day Pasco, Washington.

The reactions of Sacagawea and her baby to the hardships and hazards of the journey by horse and by canoe were not recorded by any of the explorers. In fact, she is not referred to in any journal between August 27 and October 13.

Captain Clark did record one fact about Sacagawea during the journey down the Snake River, where many natives were camped for fishing. He wrote that she made all the Indians they passed know that their intentions were friendly. "A woman with a party of men is a token of peace." By the same logic, surely a baby was also "a token of peace."

The day after the explorers started down the Columbia River, Clark had a short period of anxiety which was unconsciously relieved by Sacagawea. In order to lighten the weight in the canoes, Clark, Charbonneau, Sacagawea, and the two chiefs walked along the shore at the foot of some rapids. Clark climbed a cliff from which he could see the surrounding country. West of them, about 150 miles, stood two snow-capped peaks (now called Mount St. Helens and Mount

Hood on opposite sides of the Columbia). While sitting on a rock waiting for the others, Clark saw a crane and shot it. It fell near him. At once, several Indians whom he had seen walking on the other side of the river ran to their houses. Clark hurried down the cliff, climbed into the small canoe with three men, and crossed to the other side, his intention being to show the Indians his friendliness. On the way he shot a duck, which fell into the water. Five houses stood near the bank with doors closed and no person in sight. Pipe in hand to suggest peace, Clark opened one of the doors. Inside, thirty-two persons, chiefly women and children, were crowded together—all terrified, some crying and others wringing their hands. Clark shook hands with them in a friendly manner, as did each of his men. They were similarly friendly with terrified groups in the four other houses. Most of the people did calm down, but they refused to smoke with Clark on the cliff where he waited.

Then Captain Lewis and the rest of the party came into sight with Sacagawea sitting in one of the boats. As soon as a few of the natives saw her, they pointed to her and told those who had remained in their terrified position that a woman was in the party. Immediately all came out of their houses "and appeared to assume new life. The sight of this Indian woman . . . [assured] these people of our friendly intentions . . . no woman ever accompanied a war party in this quarter." The Indian men joined the captains, who "smoked with the people in the greatest friendship."

Through the Nez Perce chiefs, they learned that the natives had been sure that the strangers were not men but creatures fallen from the clouds. "The noise of the rifle, which they had never heard before, [was] considered merely as the sound to announce so extraordinary an event." The way that Clark lighted his pipe (with a "burning-glass") seemed to them like bringing fire from heaven. Soon natives and white men were smoking together "in great harmony."

The journey down the Columbia was even more dangerous than the journey down the Clearwater and Snake rivers. There were rapids and more rapids: one of them, two miles long, required two hours of hard paddling. There were also many islands, both small and large; many rocks, sometimes strewn across the channel, sometimes stretching along one of the walls of the river, which is narrow in places; and there were waterfalls.

Several of the many Indians along the way had advised the captains to portage around the Great Falls, the first of these cascades. (They were long known as Celilo Falls.) So the men unloaded their canoes at the head of the rapids and carried their supplies to the foot of the perpendicular waterfall of twenty feet. Indians assisted by taking some of the heavy articles by horse.

Captain Clark hauled the boats over a point of land to the water again. After a short distance in the canoes, they again landed and let the boats down eight feet, "as slowly as possible by strong ropes of elk skin . . . prepared for that purpose."

On the morning of October 24, the Nez Perce chiefs who had traveled with them down the three rivers since October 8, told the captains that they wanted to return home. They were now near enemies of their people. The captains persuaded them to travel a little farther partly because the next falls were said to be very difficult. The chiefs would be of great assistance because of their knowledge of the river.

This passage was called the Short Narrows. A huge rock stretched across the river to the hills on the other side, leaving a river channel only forty-five yards wide. The water was "thrown into whirls and swells. It boiled in every part with the greatest agitation." To the astonishment of the Indians watching the strangers, Cruzat, the principal waterman, "shot the rapids," steering the boat safely through the Short Narrows! A mile and a half farther downstream, they stopped by a very bad rapid. This time all the men who could not swim carried the most valuable of the baggage by land, while other men took the canoes, two at a time, through the whirling water. At the end of the day, they had traveled only six miles.

The Indians in the village where the Expedition stopped received the strangers with great kindness. Several invited them into their homes, and in the evening great numbers of them came to the white men's camp, including the principal chief and several warriors of the nearby nation that, according to the two Nez Perce chiefs traveling with the explorers, had been at war with their people.

These two old chiefs were now with their white friends, so the captains took advantage of the opportunity to remind all of them of the evils of war—not only the killing but also other results of fighting, such as poverty. At the end of the discussion, the captains had some reason to believe "that the war should no longer continue, and that in the future they would live in peace with each other."

They gave the chief of the nearby nation a medal and some small articles of clothing. Cruzat brought out his violin. "And our men danced, to the great delight of the Indians, who remained with us to a late hour." The next morning, the explorers traveled down a very difficult and very dangerous part of the Long Narrows. At about the same time, the two Nez Perce chiefs walked down to the village to see the men whom the captains had changed from enemies to friends. They wanted "to smoke a pipe of friendship on the renewal of peace."

Afterward, the Nez Perce chiefs went to the captains to say farewell. Lewis and Clark stopped their work to smoke "a parting pipe with their two faithful friends, who had accompanied [them] from the heads of the river." Each had bought a horse and two robes for they intended to return home by land.

The rest of that day some men hunted, some repaired the canoes, others dried the supplies in the canoes. Lewis "made the observations necessary to determine the longitude," and conferred with two village chiefs who, with their followers, visited the camp. They had brought and received gifts.

In the evening a fire was built in the middle of the camp. While the Indians sat around it, Cruzat again played his violin and the explorers danced—York among them. The Indians had such a good time that several of them decided to spend the night with the Expedition.

After this day of rest from the river, the explorers felt ready for the next difficulties. Their experiences with the rapids and in the narrows were good preparation for what the captains called "the Great Shoot." Traders and early pioneers soon made it well known as "the Cascades of the Columbia,"[6] where rocks and rapids made giant waterfalls. The river dropped sixty feet in two miles. Across the slippery rocks men again carried the baggage. In spite of care taken with the boats, three had to be repaired. It took most of two days, in the rain, to travel only seven miles.

The next day they portaged around the second of the cascades, "the last of all the descents of the Columbia." That day they met the first tide water, and later when the fog lifted on November 7, they had their first view of the Pacific Ocean. "O the joy!" wrote Captain Clark. "That ocean, the object of all our labors, the reward of all our anxieties. The cheering view exhilarated the spirits of all the party, who were still more delighted on hearing the distant roar of the breakers."

In his letter of instructions to Captain Meriwether Lewis, dated June 20, 1803, President Jefferson had begun a paragraph with these words: "Should you reach the Pacific ocean . . . ," followed by his instruction: "On your arrival on that coast, endeavor to learn if there be any port within your reach frequented by the sea vessels of any nation . . . ." Thomas Jefferson's dream of more than twenty years had come true!

6

Winter at Fort Clatsop

THE ocean was still twenty miles away, however—unusually long miles, they learned. The forested slopes beside the river were beautiful, with evergreen trees taller than any they had ever seen, trees that had trunks unbelievably large. But the weather! And the water! Fog, rain, and a penetrating dampness kept their clothing and bedding wet most of November. After a while, both rotted. Hail, thunder, and lightning were frequent, and a raw wind blew almost all of the time.

The incessant wind kept the river too rough for the men to paddle through it. "The swells were so high," wrote Captain Clark on November 8, "and the canoes rolled in such a manner as to cause several people to be very sick." Sacagawea was one of those having a first experience with sea-sickness. The misery continued for several days.

Numerous Indians had passed the explorers along the Columbia River and had visited them at their camps on its shores. One evening was noteworthy because they had no visitors. Even more Indians visited them as they neared the ocean. Some of them wore clothing that had obviously been purchased from white traders—"scarlet and blue blankets, sailor's jackets and trousers, shirts and hats." Some had muskets and pistols with tin powder flasks.

The captains had hoped to find, at the mouth of the Columbia, vessels of white traders, and so make the journey home by sea. But no ships came into view. They would have to spend the winter near the lower Columbia. There, food would be less scarce and the weather less severe than near the mountains. They hoped that some ship would come in the spring.

Soon they realized that because of the rough water of the Columbia and also the high tides of the Pacific they could not reach the ocean by boat. Captain Lewis and a few of the men went on foot to see the "Big Water." After their return, Captain Clark led the surprisingly few others who wanted to see more of the Pacific. They felt "much satisfied with their trip, beholding with astonishment the high waves dashing against the rocks of this immense ocean."

When Clark returned, he found Captain Lewis trying to purchase from one of the Chinook Indians a "robe made of two sea-otter skins, the fur of which was more beautiful than they had ever seen." Lewis offered him many things for the robe, among them some white beads, some red beads, a blanket, and a coat, but the man refused. At last he purchased the robe in exchange for a belt of blue beads worn by Sacagawea. In return, they gave her a coat of blue cloth.

Both the Indians who lived in the area and the ones camping there were busy fishing and digging wapato roots, which are often called "tule potatoes." The captains were pleased when a friendly Indian invited them into his lodge and treated them to a meal of this root. About the size of a small Irish potato, when it is "roasted in the embers until it becomes soft, it has an agreeable taste, and is a very good substitute for bread." Sacagawea, who seemed especially fond of roots, liked it very much.

Some of the many Indians living or camping near the explorers were as kindly and friendly as the natives along the rivers had been when the two Nez Perce chiefs traveled with them. Others were hostile and eager to steal whatever they could slip away from the strangers. And they charged so much for the food they were willing to sell that the captains were running short of articles of exchange.

The explorers never found a really good place to camp on the north side of the river (now Washington State) and they needed the meat of deer or elk. Inquiring of the Indians, they learned that elk were plentiful on the south side of the river (now Oregon). The hunters knew that elk are more easily killed than deer, and that elk meat is more nutritious than deer meat in winter. Besides, being larger, elk had more leather for the much-needed clothing and moccasins.

On November 24, the entire party held a council on the subject of where they should camp during the winter. Even York and Sacagawea were asked to express their preferences. Sacagawea replied that she favored "a place where there is plenty of Pota" (potatoes—that is, wapato roots).

In Clark's November 24 journal entry about this voting, he referred to Sacagawea as "Janey." He mentioned Janey only one other time—in his letter to Charbonneau after the explorers left him and his family. Perhaps Clark gave her the nickname because it was easier to pronounce and to spell than Sacagawea.

The opinion of the majority was that they should cross to the south side of the river and try to find a good hunting ground. In spite of wind and rain, they crossed over and found a place for a temporary camp. Captain Lewis and five men went out with two purposes in mind: to bring back some elk meat and to find a place suitable for their winter camp. Three others went hunting at the same time in different directions, while the rest remained around their warm fires, to mend their old clothes and to dry leather for new clothes and moccasins. At least one writer, Bernard De Voto, has implied that Sacagawea made the clothes for the men, but it seems doubtful that one woman could have done all the work of tanning deer hides to clothe 32 men. But Sacagawea surely helped.

One evening the Indian girl gave Captain Clark a piece of bread made of flour. She had kept it carefully for some time, expecting to give it to her child, Jean Baptiste. Unfortunately, it had got wet, and dampness had caused it to turn a little sour. But Clark wrote in his journal that he ate it with great satisfaction, it being the only mouthful of bread that he had eaten for many months.

Several men became ill from prolonged eating of dried fish,

so three hunters started out and three other men went up a creek in search of fresh fish or birds. One of them was successful in getting an elk, the first they had killed west of the Rocky Mountains. December 3 was a gala day. A little sunshine in the morning had "revived the spirits of the party, who were still more pleased when the elk . . . was brought into camp. It formed a most nourishing food."

Sacagawea ate the marrow out of the two shank bones of the elk and then chopped the bones fine. She then boiled the pieces of bone in water and took from the liquid a pint of grease. Clark wrote that the grease was "superior to the tallow of the animal" for oiling boots and guns.

Two days later Captain Lewis and three of his men returned to the camp, the other two having been left to guard the results of their hunt: six elk and five deer. Lewis had found a good place for the winter camp, "with a sufficiency of elk within reach."

Though within sound of the breakers in the Pacific, the new camp site was above the swampland and marshes, "thirty feet above the level of the high tide." It was near a small river, "in a thick grove of lofty pines." Captain Lewis set the men to work at once to construct their cabins and fortification for the winter.

Until the end of December most of the men were busy felling trees, splitting logs, and building their cabins. They rejoiced that the beautiful evergreen trees (now called Douglas fir) split "into excellent boards more than two feet in width." They were also glad when they found some boards already made, lying in an old Indian house.

Their neighbors, the Clatsop Indians, were kindly and friendly. Sometimes they brought a very welcome supply of roots and berries. The explorers were delighted when two of their hunters returned with the news that they had killed eighteen elk about six miles away.

But the weather gave them no cause for joy. Sergeant Gass reported in his journal: "There is more wet weather on this coast than I ever knew in any other place; during the month we have had three fair days." Captain Clark wrote: "I have not seen one pacific day since my arrival in its vicinity."

By December 11, several of the men were showing the effects of living and working in the excessive dampness. Four had very violent colds, one had dysentery, another had tumors on his legs, and two had "been injured by dislocation and straining of their limbs." Later, some men received bruises and several complained of boils. But all continued working except on an occasional day when snow and hail fell and the wind was unusually strong. In spite of all handicaps, the cabins were near enough completion for the Expedition to move in on Christmas Eve.

On Christmas day, at daylight, the captains were awakened by the discharge of firearms of all the men. This was followed by a salute, shouts, and a song that the whole party joined in beneath their leaders' windows. Everyone was cheerful. The captains gave each man a gift—some tobacco for those who used it, a handkerchief to each one who did not.

If Captain Clark had had a dry stocking to hang up, it would have been filled to overflowing. He listed seven Christmas gifts in addition to two dozen white weasel tails given to him by Sacagawea. What use he made of weasel tails (the animal is also called ermine) seems not to have been included in the journals. (The Shoshones used weasel tails as ornaments on their tippets, or short coats.)

Their Christmas dinner consisted of elk, so spoiled that they ate it only through necessity, some spoiled pounded fish, and a few roots. The day was warm. Other days had been so warm that their bountiful supply of elk had spoiled. But before New Year's Day, when the captains were again awakened by the discharge of small arms, the hunters had been successful. Their dinner consisted of fresh boiled elk and wapato roots.

During the week, they completed the circle of eight cabins. One of them was used for storage, the others for dwellings. Each door faced the center of the circle. The outer walls joined together to form a stockade as protection against an attack by hostile Indians. By sunset on December 30, the men had completed the fortification, and had named it Fort Clatsop.

They announced to their Indian visitors "that every day at

that hour the gates would be closed, and they must leave the fort and not enter it till sunrise." Fort Clatsop was now a military post, with a sentinel on guard day and night. Each of four men was on guard duty for six hours.

One group of Indian visitors grumbled at the order, but soon camped nearby. The very next day, after making a comment about those Indians, one of the captains reported, "Our new regulations, however, and the appearance of the sentinel have improved the behavior of all our Indian visitors. They left the fort before sunset, even without being ordered."

During the first week of 1806, five men were sent to the coast to make salt. Captain Lewis decided that they should spend the winter near the ocean since the seven barrels of salt with which they had started were then almost gone. In fact, they had had no salt since before Christmas. The men found a good place about fifteen miles from the fort (near present Seaside, Oregon), where they boiled down sea water and made salt "which was white, fine, and very good." They could make three or four quarts a day, and so by the end of February they had not only furnished the Expedition with their daily need but had twelve kegs of salt prepared for the homeward journey.

Their Indian neighbors treated the salt-makers kindly and gave them some of the blubber of a whale. The men brought part of the blubber with them when they returned to Fort Clatsop. They also brought stories of the whale and of neighboring Coast Indians. After being cooked, the blubber "was found to be tender and palatable, in flavor resembling the beaver." Hoping to procure some for themselves, or at least to purchase some blubber from the Indians, several of the men made ready to leave for the ocean the next morning.

Sacagawea overheard the talk about the big fish and about the men going to the ocean to see it and asked to go with them. This seems to have been her only request and the cause of her only complaint during the entire journey. She said that she had traveled a long way with the white men "to see the great waters, and that now that monstrous fish was also to be seen, she thought it very hard she could not be permitted to see either." She had never had a close view of the ocean, although she had been near it for almost a month. "So reasonable a request could not be denied: they were therefore suffered to accompany Captain Clark" when he and his men started after an early breakfast on January 6. Both Sacagawea and Charbonneau are included in each captain's account of the beginning of the journey, but Sacagawea is not mentioned again in the journals until April 16.

Only two members of the party are named in Clark's rather detailed account of the journey. It was a strenuous one, chiefly on foot. Five very long days were made bearable largely because there was no rain.

The party of twelve started in two canoes, but a high wind soon changed their plans. They found a path, followed it on foot across three marshes, crossed the deepest part of one of several creeks, first by walking on a tree that had been felled, and then by wading.

After walking along the beach for several miles, Clark hired a young Indian to guide them to the spot where the whale lay. For more than two miles they walked "over the round slippery stones at the foot of a high hill." It looked almost perpendicular. Part of it was so steep that all had to pull themselves "up about 100 feet by means of bushes and roots." It took them about two hours to climb 1,000 or 1,200 feet. Then they continued over a bad road until night, when all welcomed rest from the day's fatigue.

The next morning they climbed to the highest point of the mountain, an open spot facing the ocean. "Here one of the most delightful views in nature presents itself," wrote Clark. When they followed their guide down the mountain, they found the descent steep and treacherous. Some parts were dangerous from slippery clay, others because of "rugged, perpendicular rocks which overhang the sea." A false step would have caused any one of them to fall into the ocean. They reached the beach safely, walked two more miles, waded across another creek, and arrived at the place where the waves had swept the whale on shore.

Only its skeleton remained, about 105 feet long. All the

flesh and blubber had been taken by the Indians. In a tiny village, Captain Clark bought about 300 pounds of blubber and a few gallons of oil, paying what he thought was a very high price.

Disappointed though Clark probably was by not seeing the whale, he was able to chuckle when he wrote in his journal about the trip. Providence had been more kind to them than to Jonah, "having sent this Monster to be swallowed by us instead of swallowing us as Jonah's did."

What Sacagawea's reactions were to this scenic and difficult journey can be learned only from the sworn testimony Finn Burnett has given of what she had told him many years later (See Chapter 15). And Jean Baptiste? There seems to be no reference to him in anyone's journal for nearly a year after Clark and the little family had their terrifying experience (June 29, 1805) above the Great Falls of the Missouri. When we picture the group on their way to see the whale, we can imagine Sacagawea pushing her way through all those difficulties while carrying on her back or in her arms her baby almost eleven months old.

For a while after the journey to see the whale, most of the men were busy drying their clothes and trying to get rid of the sand fleas in them. They began the long task of making new clothes of leather, but they lacked some of the material needed in dressing the skins to make them soft enough for easy sewing. However, on February 23, the captains reported: "The men are now fully provided with leathern clothes and moccasins; being better off in this respect, indeed, than at any previous period of our journey."

During the dreary winter, there was considerable illness and recovery was slow. The men were still weak from the long and difficult journey westward, and the food, even when plentiful, was not the best for the sick. Private Gibson, it seemed for a while, would not live. Private Bratton, suffering from lumbago, was unable to walk for some time before the Expedition started homeward. Both men were reported "quite sick" in early February.

Indians from several villages along the coast visited Fort Clatsop frequently, and from them the captains learned a great variety of facts. Lewis made a scientific study of the trees and other plants of the region and made a less scientific study of the birds, animals, and fish.

Captain Clark brought his journal up-to-date, chiefly by copying some entries from Lewis. He made or improved his sketches of leaves and of wildlife and spent much of the winter preparing a map from the sketches and field notes he had made since they left Fort Mandan. The major rivers with their important tributaries and the route across the Rockies were located with their latitudes and longitudes. It was the first map ever made of the West and showed "the most direct and practicable water-communication across the continent, for the purpose of commerce," to quote from the directions of President Jefferson. Studying the map, they realized that they had made one error: they did not need to make that difficult canoe trip on the upper waters of the Missouri River. On their way eastward, they would use the overland trails that Indians had told them about.

In March, the men who were not ill became busier with preparations for the return journey. The gunsmith, using the spare parts that Lewis had been so far-sighted as to purchase, saw that all the guns were in good order. Fortunately, their powder had been stored in water-tight containers. A much needed canoe was hard to purchase, because the Indians' price was so high. At last Captain Lewis very reluctantly gave up his officer's gold-laced coat, which he seldom wore. Except for a few large items for important purchases, "two handkerchiefs would contain all the small articles of merchandise" they had left for the long eastward journey.

Because the chief of the Clatsop Indians had been "the most kind and hospitable of all the Indians" in the area of the fort, the captains gave him their houses and furnishings at Fort Clatsop, and also "a certificate of the kindness and attention [they] had had from him." They gave a certificate of the same kind to the chief of the Chinook Indians. The chiefs and some of their men had often visited and smoked with the captains, giving them much information about the coast tribes.

The captains wrote cheerfully of their experiences: "Although we have not fared sumptuously the past winter and spring at Fort Clatsop, we have lived quite as comfortably as we had any reason to expect, and have accomplished every end we had in view in staying at this place, except that of meeting any of the traders who visit this coast and the mouth of the Columbia."[7]

7
Eastward Bound

THE captains had planned to stay at Fort Clatsop until the first of April because the weather would be milder close to the ocean during winter months. Warm spring Chinook winds expected with the equinox about March 21 would melt the snow at higher elevations. When the elk retreated to the mountains, it signaled the beginning of the spring thaw and from then on elk meat would become scarce at the coast.

The explorers had made enough salt, dried enough meat and fish, made new clothing and repaired their old, repaired the guns and canoes, and since no ships had appeared from the ocean they were anxious to begin their homeward journey eastward.

So they finished their preparations for departure. When the rain stopped in the morning of March 23, they loaded their canoes and at one o'clock took leave of Fort Clatsop. Sixteen miles up the river, they found that the hunters who had been sent ahead had killed two elk. Soon they were able to buy some dogs for the invalids.

Gradually they added variety to the elk and deer meat by getting seal and sturgeon, geese and ducks and eagles, wapato and camas roots. On April 7, they decided that they had a sufficient quantity of dried meat to last them until they reached the Nez Perces—if they could occasionally get supplies of roots, dogs, and horses.

Among the many Indians who visited the explorers in the early part of their journey were two young men who said that they lived at the falls of a large river that enters the Columbia from the south. While working on his maps during the winter, Clark had wondered what river watered that large area southward. By a gift of a burning glass that pleased one of the young men, Clark persuaded him to lead eight of them up that tributary.

They soon discovered that three small islands near its mouth had concealed the largest tributary of the Columbia below the Snake River. It is now known as the Willàmette River. After measuring the depth of the water near the mouth of this tributary. Clark wrote that it appeared "to possess water enough for the largest ship." He did not know that he had selected the site of the city of Portland.

The explorers had already become acquainted with four snow-capped peaks of the Cascade Range: Rainier, St. Helens, Adams, and Hood. As they entered the Willamette River, they saw, southeast of them, a fifth high peak, "a regular cone, covered with snow." Clark promptly named it Mount Jefferson. An old Indian gave him a great deal of information about the surrounding country, and with his finger drew in the dust a map of the Willamette River and its biggest island.

Every day the explorers met numerous Indians, and many visited their camps at night, "with no object but to gratify their curiosity." Some were friendly and trustworthy. Those who were "sullen and ill-humored" soon showed themselves to be dishonest also. Most of the thievery the explorers experienced on the entire journey was in the area of the Narrows, the Cascades, and the Great Falls.

The most conspicuous object stolen was Scannon, Captain Lewis's Newfoundland dog. An Indian who spoke the Clatsop language, which the captains had learned during the winter, told them that some men of a neighboring band had taken the dog to their village. Scannon had traveled all the way from Pittsburgh to the Pacific with Captain Lewis. He had saved men from being trampled by buffaloes, he had guarded them from grizzly bears, and he was a friend of the entire party.

Three well-armed men were sent at once in pursuit of the thieves. They were ordered to fire if there was any resistance. After two miles, the white men saw the thieves. The Indians, finding themselves pursued, left the dog and hurried on.

The captains then ordered all the Indians out of their camp, and told them that whoever stole any of their baggage or insulted their men should be instantly shot. It was now necessary, the captains decided, "to depart from [their] mild and pacific course of conduct."

But the majority of the Indians they met were honest. The day before Scannon was stolen, one of the explorers' canoes got loose and drifted down the river. Indians in the village brought it back to the white men. And after the Scannon incident, the chief of a neighboring village was so ashamed of the thieves that he came to apologize and to explain that the rest of the tribe were not like those two bad men. The captains gave each of these visitors a small reward.

Travel up the Columbia, through the narrows and around the waterfalls, was even more difficult in March and April than it had been in the autumn. The water was much higher because of heavy spring rains and melting snow at low elevations. In three days in April, the Expedition had advanced not more than seven miles. While making a portage, they lost a canoe. Helpless because of wind and current, they watched their boat drift down the river.

The captains then decided to get horses to carry the baggage over land. But they had so little merchandise left that by the end of the fourth day they had bought only four horses. They were forced to pay twice as much for each of them as they had paid the Shoshones for far better ones. Sacagawea and Charbonneau went with Captain Clark one day, but they brought him no success.

A few days later, on April 20, 1806, the explorers' luck turned. An Indian with two horses not only offered to guide them as far as the Nez Perces, but also politely offered to lend one of his horses for the baggage. He was a Nez Perce himself and seemed to be a sincere and honest Indian. In a few days, they were joined by a Nez Perce family on their way home.

By April 24, they had enough horses to carry all their

baggage and also Private Bratten, who was still too sick to walk. They "therefore proceeded wholly by land." This time there is no mention of a horse for Sacagawea. Perhaps there would have been one for her if Charbonneau had not tied it so carelessly that it wandered away and could not be found.

Within a few days, the explorers were warmly welcomed by Yel-lépt, chief of the Wallawalla Indians. In October, he had invited them to visit him and his people, and the captains had promised that they would do so on their return. This time the chief invited them to stay at his village for three or four days, during which time he would supply them with food and would furnish them with horses for their journey.

Chief Yellept was a man of much influence, both among his own people and among those of neighboring tribes. His village was near the mouth of the Walla Walla River, which flows from the southeast into the Columbia a short distance below the mouth of the Snake River. As soon as the Expedition reached his village, the chief called together a large number of people. He urged all of them to treat the strangers with hospitality, and he set an example by bringing them an armful of wood and a platter containing three roasted fishes.

Next morning Chief Yellept presented Captain Clark with an excellent white horse. In appreciation, Clark gave him his sword, for which the chief had expressed a desire. Later, each of two lesser chiefs made the captains a gift of another fine horse.

Among the Wallawallas was a Shoshone woman, a prisoner, from a band south of the Willamette River. Fortunately, she and Sacagawea could understand each other. Through these interpreters, the white men conversed with the Wallawalla leaders for several hours. The Indians seemed fully satisfied, even much pleased, with the strangers and with their statements about the purposes of their exploration.

The conversation inspired the Indians with so much confidence that they brought to the gathering place several sick persons and asked for help. Captain Clark, the chief medical man, set the broken arm of one person, eased the pain of another who had rheumatism, and gave "eye-water" to many. Realizing their lack of medical knowledge, the captains were always very careful not to give the Indians anything harmful.

The captains had expected to depart after one night, but when they asked Chief Yellept for a canoe for the purpose of crossing the river, they found that he had made other plans. He had invited the people from a neighboring village to join his people in a dance for the amusement of the visitors.

Shortly before sunset, about one hundred men and some women came to his village. First the explorers danced for about an hour to the music of the violin. Then several hundred Indians—men, women and children—sang and danced at the same time. Frequently they jumped up and down, keeping time with the music. Some of the explorers danced with the crowd, "to the great satisfaction of the Indians."

The explorers were urged to stay longer, but the leaders felt that they must press on the next morning. As they were making camp the second evening after their departure, three young men from the Wallawalla village arrived with a steel trap that had been left behind by mistake. This act prompted the leaders to write a final tribute to the Wallawallas: "We may, indeed, justly affirm that, of all the Indians whom we have met since leaving the United States, the Wollawollans [*sic*] are the most hospitable, honest, and sincere."

The three young Wallawallas continued with them next day. On the following day, May 3, they were pleasantly surprised to see one of their Nez Perce friends whom they had called Bighorn because of the horn of a Rocky Mountain or bighorn sheep hanging from his left arm. The first chief of a large band of Nez Perces, he had made friends for the strangers the previous year among the Indians along the Snake River. From someone he had learned that the explorers were returning, and so, with ten of his warriors, he had set out to meet them.

He and his men turned back with the Expedition. Their arrival was fortunate, for the Nez Perce guide and the three Wallawallas had left suddenly that morning and never returned. It was good to have friends around, for the weather was a combination of rain, hail, snow, and violent wind.

The next day they reached some Nez Perce houses, and found two more of their good friends. One man was the pilot who guided them down the Clearwater and the Snake rivers to the Columbia. The other was the younger of the two chiefs who had accompanied them all the way to the Great Falls of the Columbia. They now told the explorers the shortest and best route to the fork of the Clearwater, where they would find Twisted Hair with their horses.

The first meeting with Twisted Hair was not pleasant, but the next day twenty-one of their horses, most of them in excellent condition, were brought to the explorers. By the end of May, all their horses were with them except the two that had been taken by Old Toby and his son for the rest of their journey home; they probably considered the horses as wages for their guiding services.

At every place they camped, they were joined by many Indians, often by some who lived at a distance. Once the captains learned from a visiting Shoshone, through Sacagawea, that an old man was saying that the white strangers were bad men who were probably intending to kill the Nez Perces.

In a speech translated through Sacagawea and the Shoshone visitor, Captain Lewis told the people about his country and the purposes of the visit. Earlier Bighorn had rejoined the explorers in time to help make their friendly intentions known.

Another evening they talked with three men whose home was north of the Nez Perces, at the falls of a large river that flows into the Columbia from the east. The source of the river, they learned, is a large lake in the mountains. It is now called Lake Coeur d'Alene, in northern Idaho, the source of the Spokane River that has such beautiful falls. These places were added to Clark's map. The people who lived there are now known as the Coeur d'Alene Indians. Their name for themselves is *Skitwish*; its meaning is unknown.

After a day of slippery travel over snow, on May 10, the Expedition was welcomed with ceremony and with hospitality by a Nez Perce chief and his principal men. Learning that his visitors were hungry, he had his people bring two bushels of dried roots and some dried salmon. Finding that they wanted some horse meat, he gave them "two young fat horses, without asking anything in return." Then he had a large leathern tent spread out for them and asked them to make it their home while they were in his village.

Soon a principal chief from another Nez Perce village arrived with fifty of his men. After cooking and eating a supper of horse-meat and roots, the captains spent the evening explaining who they were, telling the natives the purposes of their journey, and answering their questions. Their interpreters were Charbonneau, Sacagawea, and a Shoshone boy who was a prisoner of the Nez Perces. The atmosphere was so friendly that the tent was crowded with Indians all night.

On May 11, they were visited by other neighbors. After discovering that in their lodge were the four principal chiefs of the Nez Perces, the captains decided to hold a council with all the chiefs and their warriors. They would repeat what they had said the evening before and would explain more fully the purposes of their government, "with respect to the inhabitants of this western part of the Continent."

First they drew a map of the country on a mat with a piece of charcoal. Then they explained "the nature and power of the American nation." They emphasized its desire for peace among all the natives, and promised that trading posts would be established for the exchange of their goods with the white man's goods.

Much of the day was spent in this council, because all the speeches had to pass through five languages. One of the captains made his speech in English to one of the Frenchmen in the party, probably Labiche. In French, that man gave the information to Charbonneau, who translated it into Minnetaree for Sacagawea. She spoke in her native language to the Shoshone boy, and he passed the information on to the Nez Perces in their native language.

Captain Clark reported that "they appeared highly pleased." One young Nez Perce was so gratified that he brought a gift to Lewis and Clark—"a very fine mare with a colt." He asked the captains to accept the gift as a proof that he would follow their advice. His heart had been made glad, he said, by what they had told his people. The following morning, two young men gave each of the captains a good horse, and the captains responded with gifts to them and to the chiefs.

Before the council with the chiefs and warriors had ended, many patients were waiting for medical attention. Most of them were afflicted with sore eyes, or rheumatism, or a disorder that the captains thought was caused by their diet of roots. A few had other troubles. Captain Clark had won his reputation as "the favorite physician" a few days earlier when he had relieved a man of the pain in his knee and had treated the abscess on a woman's back, her husband having promised to give Clark a horse if he would help her. The following morning, the husband brought Captain Clark the horse, for his wife had slept better than she had for some time. In the autumn, the medical services had been free. But now, needing food and having only a few articles to exchange for it, they charged a fee. The Nez Perces had many dogs and horses and did not eat them. So the explorers soon had plenty of food, even when their hunters had no luck.

The morning after the council with the captains, the chiefs and their warriors met to discuss the matter of trading posts. They ended by voting their approval. As was their custom, they then held a second council. Captain Lewis attended it, leaving Captain Clark with the people who needed medical assistance. The meeting was opened by the aged father of one of the chiefs. Lewis was told that the snow was still so deep in the mountains that they should not attempt to start until after the next full moon. The Indians recommended a camping place across the river, a few miles away, and offered to assist them with a canoe for their baggage.

The next afternoon, after the captains finished their medical care, the men moved the camp. The site that had been recommended was an excellent one, in the area of the present village of Kamiah, on the Clearwater River. It was near game and also near the salmon that was expected to come up from the Pacific soon. Also, one of the chiefs who had many horses gave them permission to kill one at any time. They stayed for nearly a month at this camping place, from May 14 until June 10.

In the middle of May several of the explorers complained of headache and colic, but they became much better after eating some of the roots gathered by Sacagawea. The captains called them fennel roots, which are similar to carrots. She gathered a quantity of them, and they made a pleasant and nourishing addition to the meat. She also found onions in abundance, which were boiled with the meat.

The following week, Jean Baptiste, the youngest member of the Expedition became ill. This sturdy little fellow had traveled in damp canoes up and down rivers, and on horse-back over slippery rocks on steep mountain slopes, and he had shared exposure to rain, snow, and cold winds. Twice he had escaped drowning. But while cutting teeth the child developed a high fever, both captains reported on May 22. He had had several days of serious diarrhea, and his throat and neck were very swollen. They gave him a dose of cream of tartar and sulphur and applied a poultice of hot onions to his neck several times that day and the following night. The next two days he was reported to be even worse, and it was not until May 27 that he was said to be "much better," and even then his neck was swollen. A week later, Captain Clark applied some salve to his throat made of a mixture of the resin of long-leafed pine, beeswax, and bear's oil. On June 8, the child was "nearly recovered."

Lewis and Clark seemed much concerned about Jean Baptiste. For eighteen successive days, each of them wrote at least a brief report of his condition. Strangely, except for one reference to "the child of Sacagawea," there is no mention of the baby's mother.

During his weeks with the Nez Perces, Clark often treated forty sick or injured Indians in one day. "The extent of our medical fame is not a little troublesome," he once lamented in his journal.

By using the Indian sweat bath, he brought relief to Private Bratton, whose back still troubled him so much that he could not "walk or even sit upright without much pain." On the advice of Private Shields, the captains gave Bratton a steam bath as hot as he could endure and then plunged him into cold water twice and returned him to the steam bath. During both steam baths, he drank large amounts of horse-mint tea. When they removed him the second time, they carefully wrapped him and allowed him to cool slowly. The next morning, he was able to walk slowly and was nearly free from pain and continued to gain strength very quickly.

In the last days of May and the first of June, the hunters and several others were busy securing food for the trip over the Rocky Mountains. They were determined not to suffer from hunger in the cold of the mountains as they had suffered on the journey westward. Sacagawea was busy gathering fennel roots and drying them. Clark wrote that the roots were about the size of a man's finger, that they were palatable, whether fresh, roasted, or boiled.

When Chief Cut-nose and ten or twelve warriors came for a farewell visit, the captains exchanged three of their poorer horses for excellent ones. The men must have been in high spirits, for after the business was finished, they and the Indians ran several foot-races. Then they "divided themselves into two parties and played prison base." The captains were pleased, not only because of the fun, but also because of the vigorous exercise that several men needed before beginning the long journey.

One of the Nez Perces advised them not to start eastward "before the next full moon"—about the first of July. Earlier than that, he said, there would not be grass for the horses on top of the mountains. Other Indians thought that they could start earlier, and the explorers were eager to do so. Planning ahead, the captains realized that they should leave Fort Mandan for St. Louis before ice formed in the Missouri River.

Three of the chiefs whom they knew best made their last calls on the captains on June 8 and 9. They and their people were leaving for a meeting of the whole Nez Perce nation, and so the captains said farewell to men whom they considered among the best-natured and most likable they had ever known. They were calm, gentle, and honest.

8

The Explorers Separate

THE men were in high spirits in early June because they would be starting soon. They amused themselves in the afternoons with different games. All were pleased that they had plenty of horses, "most of them fine, strong, active horses, in excellent condition." Each person had one to ride and a smaller one for luggage; there were additional ones in case of accident or want of food.

On June 10, they traveled toward Camas Prairie and camped near where they had first met the Nez Perces in the autumn of 1805. This time they saw the camas in full bloom, and the many acres of blue blossoms looked like blue lakes. They continued on over roads made slippery by rain, up through thick growths of pine trees, over fallen timber, through deep snow, up high hills and down deep ravines, seeing beautiful wildflowers, many kinds of birds, and even the nest of a hummingbird. The nights were extremely cold.

On June 16, they came to the place on Hungry Creek where Captain Clark had hung some horse meat for the main party the previous September. There they spent the night so that the horses could graze in the plentiful grass. The next morning they crossed the creek with difficulty and danger, for the water was deep and rapid. They followed the creek up a mountain for three miles—and suddenly found themselves "enveloped in snow from 12 to 15 feet in depth, even on the south side." The air was keen and cold, no vegetation was in sight, and their hands and feet felt numb. The snow was hard enough for the horses to walk on safely, but no one could see the road.

At once they realized some of the hazards of trying to go farther. There would be dangers not only to themselves and their horses, but also to their very valuable records and scientific collections. After discussing their problem, they carefully stored everything they would not need for a few days and then rode back to camp beside a place where there was grass. Sergeant Gass wrote in his journal that they "turned back melancholy and disappointed."

Next morning Droulliard and Shannon were sent back to the Nez Perces to hasten the three young men who had promised to go with the explorers, or to find some others who would guide them over the mountains back to Traveler's-rest Creek.

Sergeant Gass had other melancholy facts to report during the next five days: a man accidentally cut himself with a sharp knife, one of the horses fell and rolled over its rider, mosquitoes were troublesome in the evening, there was not enough fresh food, in spite of all efforts. When Drouillard and Shannon failed to return, the captains, at least, grew concerned.

Sacagawea was not mentioned in the explorers' journals between May 18 and July 1, when they were along the upper Clearwater River, where she was digging and drying fennel roots. How did she manage to take care of a seventeen-months-old boy in air so keen and cold that even the men's hands and feet were numb?

But on June 22, life began to brighten. Hunters were surprisingly successful: they brought back eight deer and three bears. The next afternoon Droulliard and Shannon returned, bringing with them three young Nez Perces who promised to go with the explorers as far as the Great Falls of the Missouri—for a fee of two guns. The captains knew that all three of the men were "of good character, respected in the nation."

When they reached the place where they had stored their baggage, they found everything safe. Since the explorers left there, the snow had melted four feet. The next day, at a high spot in the mountains, the captains felt so enclosed by their surroundings that escape seemed impossible. Although they had been there less than ten months before, they doubted that they could find their way without their Indian guides.

Their guides did not hesitate—wherever the snow had disappeared, they saw the road. When the horses were badly in need of food, the Nez Perces promised that they would soon reach grass in abundance, and their promises were fulfilled.

By June 29, the Expedition had left the snow behind, and early in the afternoon they reached the warm springs near present-day Missoula, Montana. The largest spring, which the Indians had "formed into a bath by stopping the run with stone and pebbles," had the hottest water. Both the explorers and the Indians had the fun of bathing in the springs. Captain Lewis, with difficulty, remained in the hottest water for nineteen minutes—and sweated much afterward. The Indians, according to their custom, stayed in the hot water as long as they could and then plunged into the icy water of Traveler's-rest Creek. This procedure they repeated several times, ending with a bath in one of the warm springs.

The next evening the explorers and their guides reached the mouth of Traveler's-rest Creek, where they had camped on September 8 and 9 the previous year. There they again stayed two days, to refresh themselves and their horses, to get some meat and dry it, and also to see that all their weapons were in good order.

The captains had decided that the Expedition would separate, in order to explore a larger area than they had on their way west. Lewis and his men would travel northward by the shortest route their guides knew to the Great Falls. Then they would explore the area north of the Missouri, along the Marias River. Captain Clark and his party would start southward, retracing their steps until they reached the Three Forks. Then they would travel eastward to the Yellowstone

River and down it in order to explore the largest tributary of the Missouri. Both of these main parties would be subdivided, for different duties, during the explorations. The captains planned that all would unite at the junction of the Yellowstone and the Missouri, near what is now the western boundary of North Dakota.

Although the Nez Perce guides were eager to leave, they were persuaded to travel with Lewis's party for a day or two, to show them the shortest road to the Missouri. The explorers expressed their appreciation in two ways. Some of the young men and the guides amused themselves by running races, on foot and with horses. In both of these, the Indians "proved themselves hardy, athletic, and active."

To the one who was the son of a chief, Captain Lewis gave a small medal and a gun. The Indian was so pleased he asked that the two exchange names. An Indian could give no greater gift than his own name and Lewis was given a name that means "White Bearskin Folded." Chief Cameahwait of the Shoshones had given his name to Captain Clark months before.

Captain Clark's party consisted of twenty men, Sacagawea and her baby—and Captain Lewis's dog. Charbonneau would interpret with the Crow Indians, Sacagawea with the Shoshones. With fifty horses, they started south up what is now called the Bitterroot River. Their first goal was the place where they had left some canoes and baggage the previous August. As their second day was the Fourth of July, Captain Clark and his party "halted at an early hour for the purpose of doing honor to the birthday of our nation's independence."

Sacagawea made one of her two contributions to the guiding of the Lewis and Clark Expedition two afternoons later. They had been following a road traveled by the Flathead Indians, a much better and shorter road than the one they had traveled in the autumn. When they came out onto a broad level plain, the tracks of the Indians scattered so much that they could no longer be followed. "But Sacagawea recognized the plain at once." She told Clark that she had been there often in her childhood. It was a favorite place of her people for gathering camas and other roots and for taking beaver from the many creeks. When they reached the higher part of the plain, said Sacagawea, they would see a gap in the mountains through which they should pass on the way to the canoes. From that gap, now called Gibbon's Pass, they would see a high mountain covered with snow.

Clark followed Sacagawea's directions, and on July 8 they reached the Two Forks of the Jefferson River, where they had stored the baggage and supplies they left behind, including chewing tobacco. The men who chewed tobacco had been without it for months, and for some time they had also been without the bark that they had used as a substitute. So eager were they to chew again "that they scarcely took the saddles from their horses before they ran to the cave and were delighted at being able to resume this fascinating indulgence." Happily, they chewed and chewed and chewed.

They found their goods safe, though a little damp, and one of their canoes leaked. The next morning all the men were busy repairing the canoes, drying everything that needed drying, and preparing for departure next day.

Sacagawea, as usual, examined the plants, and she soon found some roots that were eaten by the Indians. The stem, leaf, and rest of the plant, which grew in moist soil, resembled the common carrot in form, size, and taste, although the color was a paler yellow. Again Sacagawea made a nutritious addition to the food supply of the explorers.

On July 10, the men loaded the boats, in spite of frost-covered ground. Captain Clark divided his party into two groups: one would descend the Jefferson River with the canoes and the baggage; the others, including Clark, would ride horseback along the riverbanks and then across to the Yellowstone River. On the way they saw many animals—numerous beavers and otters in the river, deer in the bushes nearby, and antelope and bighorn sheep on the higher slopes, so there was no scarcity of food.

Exactly one week after Sacagawea had been helpful in guiding the party with Clark, she was again able to give him some useful advice. They had passed the Three Forks of the Missouri, near which she had been captured, and were in the area of the Gallatin River. Clark saw roads leading to two passes in the mountains. "The Indian woman who has been of great service to me as a pilot through this country," wrote Clark, "recommends a gap in the mountains more south, which I shall cross." The gap or pass is in a ridge that separated the explorers from the valley of the Yellowstone River. It has long been known as the Bozeman Pass, near the site of Livingston, Montana. Many years later, the Northern Pacific Railway was built across the mountains where Sacagawea had advised that the explorers cross.

As Clark and his party traveled through an open plain on their way to the pass, they saw "in every direction the roads made by the buffalo, as well as some old signs of them." Sacagawea told them that a few years before, the buffalo had been numerous, not only in those plains and valleys, but even as high as the sources of the Jefferson River. But lately they had disappeared.

Shortly after riding through the pass recommended by Sacagawea, they reached the Yellowstone River, "already a bold, rapid, and deep stream." By this time the horses' feet had become very sore from walking over sharp rocks. So the men made moccasins of green buffalo hide for the horses, which relieved them very much in crossing the plains.

Since the Nez Perce guides departed with Lewis, Clark and his men had had only a glimpse of one Indian. But on July 18, smoke was observed in the mountains. On that day Private Gibson was wounded in an accident, and soon found it extremely painful to ride. Because he would be more comfortable in a canoe than on a horse, Clark and two other men went ahead to look for timber suitable for building canoes. Finding none suitable for large crafts, Clark had two small ones made and then tied them together.

Some of the men cut down trees and worked until dark making the canoes. The hunters went out and returned with a deer, an elk, and two buffalo, while the rest of the party dressed skins for clothes.

The horses, being very tired, were turned out to rest for a few days. But the next day, twenty-four of them were missing. For three days men looked for them in every direction. On the third day, Sergeant Pryor found, near their camp, a piece of a robe and an old moccasin that looked as if it had been left but a few hours before. Another man told Clark that he had followed the trails of horses and decided that they had been driven down the river very rapidly. There was no hope of recovering them. That evening wolves or dogs stole most of the dried meat from the place where it was hanging.

By noon of July 23, the two canoes were completed and were lashed together, and everything was prepared for setting out early the next morning. Sergeant Pryor and two other men were directed to take the remaining horses overland to the Mandan villages, where they would probably be of value in trading. Soon the men learned that Pryor needed a fourth man. The horses had been so well trained by their former owners that those without riders surrounded herds of buffalo successfully. A fourth man was added to ride ahead and drive all the buffalo from the route.

In the afternoon, Captain Clark left his horse in order to examine a remarkable rock on the south side of the Yellowstone River. It is about two hundred feet high, and only one side could be climbed, for the other sides were almost perpendicular cliffs. As he scrambled towards the flat top, Clark examined the Indian carvings of figures of animals and other objects and then carved his name and the date:

W^m. Clark

July 25th. 1806

The inscription is still legible because of the iron grating that protects it from tourists.

Clark greatly enjoyed the vast view from the top—as have many people since his day. He named the rock Pompey's

Pillar, in honor of the little son of Sacagawea and Charbonneau. "My boy Pomp" appears in the letter Clark wrote to
Charbonneau after the exploring party had left the Mandans.

On July 27 the explorers took their last look at the Rocky
Mountains, which had been constantly in view since the first
of May. As they paddled down the Yellowstone, they were
sometimes stopped by the great herds of buffalo crossing the
river. They saw many elk, and also saw and heard many
wolves barking at both the elk and the buffalo. Grizzly bears
were numerous and fierce. Rattlesnakes were large and
aggressive, but luckily no one was bitten.

As the explorers approached the junction of the Yellowstone and Missouri rivers, the worst pests were the mosquitoes.
They were so troublesome that few men could close their eyes
during the night of August 2. Although Lewis's dog was in a
tent, he was bitten so much that he howled with pain. To
escape the mosquitoes, they all got up at dawn and made an
early start.

Needing meat, Clark went ashore to shoot a bighorn sheep.
But the numerous mosquitoes bit him so much that he could
not shoot with accuracy. In the afternoon, the explorers made
camp at the junction of the two rivers, at a point where they
had camped April 26, 1805.

But the next morning "the camp became absolutely unin-
habitable" because of the mosquitoes. The hunters could not
hunt. The men could not prepare the skins for making the
clothes they needed. Poor little Pomp's face was swollen and
pink—all from the bites of mosquitoes.

Captain Clark decided to go farther down the river to wait
for Captain Lewis and his party. He wrote a note and stuck it
on a pole at the junction of the Yellowstone River with the
Missouri. After reloading their canoes, the men started down
the Missouri, retracing the first part of Sacagawea's journey
with the Expedition.

At the sand-bar where they camped that evening, the
mosquitoes seemed more prevalent than usual. On shore the
next morning, Clark tried to shoot a bighorn sheep, but he
could not keep a multitude of mosquitoes "from the barrel of
his rifle long enough to take aim." He did succeed in killing a

large white bear, and the hunters killed a number of deer, only two of which were fat enough for good eating. But they did have meat—at last!

Wet from severe rain the night of August 6, they traveled down the river the next day, through intervals of rain and high wind until, in the evening, they camped at another sand-bar. There they had a violent wind for two hours, which left the air clear and cold, so that the pesky mosquitoes were completely blown away. At last, a comfortable night of sleep.

9

The Explorers Reunite and Return

ON August 8, Captain Clark and his party were astonished to see Sergeant Pryor and his three men paddling down the Missouri behind them, in skin canoes. Where were the horses they were expected to take to the Mandan villages?

The second morning after they left Captain Clark, the men had been amazed by not being able to find a single one of the horses. They examined the neighborhood of the camp and then followed the tracks of Indians and horses for ten miles. Knowing that they could never overtake the thieves on foot, they returned to their camp, packed their baggage to carry on their backs, and started toward the Yellowstone. When they reached the river near Pompey's Pillar, they made two canoes out of the skin of a buffalo that they had killed. They had seen such canoes among the Mandans and their neighbors—a frame-work of sticks with a skin tied around it. They were surprised at their feeling of safety even when they passed through the rapids of the Yellowstone in strong winds.

Clark realized at once that the explorers needed some dry skins for trading to take the place of merchandise and horses. They would want to purchase corn and beans when they reached the Mandans, and he knew that those Indians had many uses for dried skins. The hunters in the party killed deer and elk. The following day, while some men dried those skins, the hunters could find only antelope and one deer.

Search for vegetation was more rewarding. Clark found a species of cherry which he had never seen before. Some men dug quantities of roots sometimes called white-apple, which they boiled and ate with their meat. Sacagawea brought Clark a large gooseberry, rich crimson in color and delicious in taste, and also deep purple berries, a variety of currant.

The party continued to move slowly down the Missouri River. About noon on August 12, they were overjoyed to see Captain Lewis's boats come into sight. But their joy was changed to alarm when the boats neared the shore, because they did not see Captain Lewis. They learned that he was lying in one of the boats because he had suffered a gunshot wound the day before. Captain Clark immediately removed the bullet and dressed the wound, but the pain was so great that Captain Lewis fainted.

The whole party rejoiced that they were together again for the first time in nearly six weeks. They left the skin-boats, and all went together in the canoes. Soon the wind became strong, and rain began to fall, so in a short time they stopped for the night. Too stiff and sore to leave the boat, Captain Lewis spent an uncomfortable night where he had lain for more than twenty-four hours.

That evening Clark and his men learned about a journey that had been more difficult than theirs. The three Nez Perces left Lewis's party at the end of their second day of guiding. They were really afraid to go farther, and afraid for the explorers to go farther. The very thought of meeting the Minnetarees terrified them. They showed Lewis two routes to the Great Falls, and then bade the white men an affectionate farewell. Having good horses and a plentiful supply of buffalo meat, the party reached the Great Falls in ten days. Then their troubles began. Captain Lewis assigned certain duties to Sergeant Gass and five others and directed them to meet him at the mouth of the Marias River, with canoes.

Then with Droulliard and two other men, Lewis started forth to explore the valley of the Marias River. Along this northern tributary of the Missouri, he hoped to find specimens to add to the collection he was taking to President Jefferson. In that valley they had the only dangerous struggle

with Indians on the entire trip. The four white men spent a
peaceful evening conversing, in the sign language, with eight
Minnetarees and Blackfeet. Near dawn, they were awakened
by the Indians' stealing their guns, because the night watch-
man had become careless for a short time. In the struggles
that followed, two white men killed two of the Indians, and
the remaining six escaped.

But Lewis knew that he and his men must hurry away at
once. The six Indians, he felt sure, would return as soon as
possible with warriors from one or both tribes. He and his
men rode even in the moonlight, stopping only for food and a
little sleep. They became so saddle-sore that they could hardly
stand, but they rushed on when they heard shots that they
knew came from army rifles.

From the bluffs above the Missouri they saw canoes with
Sergeant Ordway and his sub-division of Captain Clark's
party. Lewis and his men released their horses, threw their
saddles into the river, and hurried into the canoes. Then the
oarsmen moved as rapidly as possible to the mouth of the
Marias River, where Sergeant Gass and his men joined them.

Lewis knew that his fifteen men had weapons far better
than those of the Indians, but he realized that there was still
danger of an attack. And so they hastened down the Missouri —
a far easier journey than they had had when paddling against
the current in 1804 and 1805. At the junction of the Yellowstone with the Missouri, they found evidences that Clark and
his party had been there, and so they pressed on.

They did stop two days to repair the canoes and to prepare
some skins for clothing. Since they left the Rockies, they had
had no time to make clothes, so "the greater part of the men
were almost naked." Mosquitoes were still pests, as they had
been to Captain Clark and his men.

From the river on August 11, Captain Lewis noticed a
herd of elk among some willows, and he landed with Private
Cruzat to hunt. Each of them shot one elk and then reloaded
their guns and went in different directions before firing
again. Just as Lewis was taking aim at an elk, a ball struck him
in his left thigh, piercing the flesh and grazing his right thigh.

Cruzat, who had poor eyesight, had thought that the brown figure in the bushes was a deer.

Painfully, Lewis reached the boat, where Sergeant Gass helped him remove his leather breeches and the bullet. Lewis dressed his own wounds, which were bleeding badly, and then lay down in the canoe. When Cruzat arrived and learned that he had shot his captain, he was greatly distressed. About one o'clock the next day, Lewis and his men "joined their friends and companions under the command of Captain Clark."

The following day, assisted by the wind and their oars, the Expedition, united again, traveled eighty-six miles. The air was cool, and the mosquitoes no longer troubled them. As they approached "the grand village of the Minnetarees" on August 14, a great crowd of people had already gathered to watch them pass. The explorers saluted them several times by firing a blunderbuss.

When they landed at the next village, they found that another crowd had gathered to welcome their return. Two chiefs expressed great joy at seeing them again, and so did all the Indian inhabitants of the Mandan village of Chief Big White.

From there Charbonneau was sent with an invitation for the Minnetarees to visit them. Droulliard was sent to the lower village to bring the Frenchman, René Jussome, who had been their interpreter with the Mandans in the winter of 1804–1805. In the meantime, Captain Clark smoked and ate with Chief Big White, called "Sha-ha-ka" by Indians.

Great numbers of Indians visited the explorers at their camp; some came to renew their acquaintance and others wanted to exchange robes or other articles for the skins the men had prepared for that purpose. People from four villages brought bushels of corn. One gift was so large that the canoes of the explorers could not hold all of it.

Because of Captain Lewis's weakness and pain, Captain Clark was kept busy with formal smoking of the peace pipe, informal conversations with the chiefs through the interpreters, and formal addresses to chiefs and warriors in different villages. The interpreters, also, must have been kept busy.

In each formal address, Captain Clark repeated his invitation to the chiefs to go with the white men to the United States to see the Great Father. But each time he was told that they could not go because of the danger of attack on their people. A warring tribe had killed several and had stolen some of their horses since the first visit of the white men.

But in the afternoon before their departure, Jussome helped the chiefs of a Mandan village to reach a different decision. They decided that the principal chief, Big White,[8] should go with the Expedition. His wife and son would go with him and also Jussome and his family.

Charbonneau would have been glad to accept the captains' invitation to go with them if the Minnetaree chiefs had been willing to go. Without them, he could no longer be useful. He knew no one in the United States, he said, and knew no way of earning a living there. He must continue in the way he had been living and would remain among the Indians. In his final report in Washington, in January 1807, Captain Lewis wrote this comment about Charbonneau: "A man of no peculiar merit. Was useful as an interpreter only, in which capacity he discharged his duties with good faith. . . ." "This man has been very serviceable to us," wrote Captain Clark on August 17, 1806, "and his wife was particularly useful among the Shoshones. Indeed, she has borne with a patience truly admirable the fatigues of so long a route encumbered with the charge of an infant, who is even now only 19 months old. We therefore paid Charbonneau wages, amounting to $500.33, including the price of a horse and a lodge [tent] purchased of him." No wages were paid to Sacagawea.

Captain Clark offered to take their "little son, a beautiful, promising child." Both parents would have been willing if he had been weaned. (Sacagawea's decision or Charbonneau's?) In a year he would be old enough to leave his mother, they said. If Captain Clark was then willing, the parents would take the boy to him to be raised in the way Clark thought proper. Clark agreed. Later, in 1808 when the boy was taken to Clark in St. Louis, Sacagawea remained with him.

So the explorers said farewell to Sacagawea, Charbonneau, and Jean Baptiste. Then they paddled down to the Mandan village of Chief Big White, where all the Indian chiefs were saying farewell to him. The chief sent his wife and son on board, accompanied by Jussome and his wife and two children. Many of the chief's people wept aloud at his going. Once more Captain Clark was asked to smoke with the principal chiefs of all the villages. They asked him to take good care of Chief Big White, "who would report whatever their Great Father should say." A final farewell was a salute from a gun in one of the canoes. Then the other Indian chiefs and the white explorers parted for the last time.

On September 9, Captain Clark wrote in his journal: "My worthy friend, Capt. Lewis, has entirely recovered. His wounds are healed up, and he can walk and even run nearly as well as he ever could."

A few nights later they camped beside a retired army officer who was starting out on a trading trip. He told them that they "had long been given up by the people of the United States generally, and almost forgotten." Only President Jefferson still had hopes for them. Jefferson wrote Lewis that he had received his letter of September 23 "with unspeakable joy. . . . The unknown scenes in which you were engaged & the length of time without hearing of you had begun to be felt awfully."

On September 23, the Expedition "descended to the Mississippi and rounded to St. Louis, . . . and having fired a salute, went on shore and received the heartiest and most hospitable welcome from the whole village." With the explorers were their valuable journals, in tin boxes safe from dampness. The captains' journals had not only accounts of their long journey, but also accounts of the geography, the plant life, and the animal life of the vast area. In the journals also were studies of the customs and the languages of several Indian tribes, which anthropologists today still value as the first reports on the North American Indians.

The leaders of the Corps of Discovery had carried out the wishes of their third partner in the exploration—President Jefferson. A tin box held Clark's maps that showed the route of the Corps of Discovery from the Mississippi River to the Pacific Ocean, with his sketches of leaves, fish, and animals. Other boxes contained botanical and zoological specimens that would please the president and would be of value to scientists in Philadelphia. The seeds of unfamiliar plants brought to Jefferson probably gave him pleasure during the remaining twenty years of his life.

In the letter that Captain Lewis wrote in St. Louis to President Jefferson, on September 23, 1806, he reported that the total distance from the mouth of the Missouri River to the Pacific Ocean and back again was 7,689 miles. The Expedition had traveled 340 miles by land, 200 of them "along a good road and 140 over tremendous mountains which for 60 miles are covered with eternal snows." In the years to come ten states were mapped and added to the Union in the territory explored by Lewis and Clark: Missouri, Kansas, Nebraska, Iowa, South Dakota, North Dakota, Montana, Idaho, Washington, and Oregon.

The United States has never had a more remarkable or a more praiseworthy exploration than the Lewis and Clark Expedition. Its great success in spite of many difficulties was largely due to its leaders, who were courageous and resourceful, self-disciplined and far-sighted, and able to deal with men, whether white or Indian. Each had unusual intelligence, broad interests, integrity, and was devoted to a worthy cause.

Sacagawea's major contribution to the Expedition, aside from her ability as interpreter, was her womanly presence with her son—a morale builder in difficult times and a symbol of peace to the Indians everywhere. A generation ago, in 1941, James Truslow Adams, distinguished scholar in American history, named Sacagawea one of the six most important American women.[9] Sacagawea's courage and loyalty were without doubt significant factors in making it possible for the Lewis and Clark Expedition to succeed in fulfilling President Jefferson's dream.

PART II: Sacagawea in Historical Perspective

10
Nearly a Century of Neglect

AFTER the triumphant return of the Expedition, both Lewis and Clark became too busy with other important assignments to prepare their carefully kept journals for publication. Early in 1807, when Lewis reported to President Jefferson on the Expedition, he was appointed Governor of the Louisiana Territory. He resigned his commission and, after representing the President at the treason trial of Aaron Burr, moved to St. Louis to begin his new—and difficult—duties.

In February of the same year, Clark was appointed Brigadier General of the Louisiana Territory and Superintendent of Indian Affairs. In January 1808, he married, took up residence in St. Louis, and soon became occupied with the Indians and with events that would eventually lead to the war of 1812.[10] After the death of Lewis under mysterious circumstances in October 1809 the entire responsibility for the journals fell to Clark. For some time he worked to get all the necessary material together, and then asked Nicholas Biddle, a Philadelphia lawyer, to edit it.[11]

Biddle selected portions from both journals and rewrote them to form a smooth-flowing narrative. He was assisted at times by George Shannon, who was studying law in Philadelphia. Perhaps it was Shannon who heard the *j* sound in the pronunciation of "Sacagawea." There is no "j" in any of the eight spellings of her name in the captains' journals. Usually she was referred to as simply "the Indian woman."

Other circumstances intervened to further delay the publication of the journals. The Philadelphia botanist who had promised to prepare the scientific notes died before he had barely begun work. A year after Biddle had finished his rewriting, he wrote Clark that the printer he had engaged had gone bankrupt, and that he himself had been elected to the Pennsylvania Legislature and had missed its session the previous winter because of his desire to supervise the printing. With some difficulty, Biddle found a publisher and, finally, in 1814 two small volumes were printed. Unfortunately, the publisher was such a poor businessman that few copies were sold. Even William Clark, then Governor of the Missouri Territory, had trouble acquiring a copy in St. Louis.

Decades later, in 1891 publisher and bookseller Francis Harper asked Dr. Elliott Coues if he would prepare a new edition of Biddle's rewritten version of the Journals of Lewis and Clark. Coues was very well qualified for the work. As an Army surgeon, he had held posts in several parts of the West. He was interested in wildlife and had written three books about birds, including *Birds of the Northwest.* He was also interested in history, was a good writer, and "had traveled more than a thousand miles of the Lewis and Clark Route." After a little persuasion, Coues accepted Harper's offer. The two small volumes became larger as Coues added informative notes about the geography and the natural history of the region. He himself retraced many miles of the Lewis and Clark trail, not marked as it is today, and he gathered information from people who were well acquainted with their own area.

After he had taken his manuscript to the publisher, Coues was given the opportunity to use the original journals of Lewis and Clark. From them he added many other notes to his manuscript. Coues' *History of the Expedition Under the Command of Lewis and Clark* was first published in 1893. It is interesting reading, and it was excellent preparation for the centennial celebrations to be held about ten years later.

Not all the facts about Sacagawea given in the original journals are included in Coues' volumes, but she is mentioned thirty-two times, in the narrative and in the footnotes. The first footnote certainly would arouse interest in her. It includes the first mention of Charbonneau, who "would have been a minus function . . . in comparison with his wife, Sacajawea, the wonderful 'Bird woman,' who contributed a full man's share to the success of the Expedition, besides taking care of her baby."

In 1904–1906, exactly a century after the Expedition, the *Original Journals of Lewis and Clark* were published for the first time. They were prepared for publication by Reuben G. Thwaites, Secretary of the Historical Society of Wisconsin, an experienced historian and author. Fortunately Thomas Jefferson had preserved most of the invaluable original documents by depositing them in the vault of the American Philosophical Society in Philadelphia, where they had lain, forgotten and unknown, for nearly seventy-five years.

The first six of the eight volumes published by Thwaites contain the daily journals of the two captains, many "sketch maps" by Captain Clark, and many notes by the editor. Volume 7 begins with the entries of Sergeant Charles Floyd and includes the journal of Private Joseph Whitehouse, which ends on November 6, 1805. It also contains about eighty letters written or received by Lewis or by Clark, which were loaned to Thwaites by relatives of the explorers. Volume 8 contains fifty-four maps by Captain Clark.

Among the letters loaned by Julia Clark Voorhis is one that her grandfather, Captain Clark, wrote to Charbonneau on August 20, 1806, while seated in the pirogue, near a village of the Arikaras, a few miles below the Mandan village that the explorers had left three days earlier. Perhaps it weighed on Clark's conscience that Sacagawea had received nothing in return for her services to the exploration. For ease in reading, we have taken the liberty of correcting Clark's spelling, punctuation, and paragraphing. He was a man of many abilities, but writing was not one of them.

You have been a long time with me and have conducted yourself in such a manner as to gain my friendship. Your woman, who accompanied you on that long, dangerous, and fatiguing route to the Pacific and back deserved a greater award for her attention and service than we had in our power to give at the Mandans.

As to your little son (my boy Pomp), you well know my fondness for him and my anxiety to take and raise him as my own child . . . .

Then he made some suggestions about Charbonneau's future, generously offering to assist him:

If you wish to live with white people . . . , I will give you a piece of land and will furnish you with horses, cows, and hogs. . . . If you wish to return as an interpreter for the Minnetarees . . . , I will get the place for you. Or if you wish to return to trade with the Indians and will bring your little son Pomp with you, I will assist you with merchandise and become myself concerned with you in trade on a small scale. . . .
If you are disposed to accept either of my offers, and will bring down your son, your famn [wife] Janey had best come along with you to take care of the boy until I get him. . . . Come prepared to accept . . . what you may choose after you get here.

(Only once in the *Journals* is Sacagawea referred to as "Janey." On November 24, 1805, Clark wrote: "After a record of the vote of the men as to the location of the winter quarters near the mouth of the Columbia, . . . Janey ["Sacajawea?"—Thwaites] [voted] in favor of a place where there is plenty of Pots [potatoes].")

Captain Clark's letter to Charbonneau is in Volume 7 of the Thwaites' edition of the journals. How Clark's granddaughter obtained the letter is not known. It is noteworthy that he made no reference to the other Shoshone wife of Charbonneau or to any child they may have had. Very likely, Clark never saw her after that brief visit at Fort Mandan on November 11, 1804, and, having been with many Indians since that day, he very likely had forgotten her.

In October 1904, Clark's letter to Charbonneau was published in the *Century Magazine*. It surely increased the interest in Sacagawea that had already been stirred by Elliot Coues' volumes. In June, Thwaites had published an article in *Scribner's Magazine* that included some passages from the journals of Lewis and Clark and some letters from the two captains, in order to suggest their personalities.

An Oregon novelist also helped prepare the country for the centennial celebrations of the Expedition. She was Eva Emery Dye, well-known in the Northwest for her historical novel, *McLoughlin and Old Oregon*, published in 1900. In 1902 she wrote a second novel, *The Conquest: The True Story of Lewis and*

Clark. In her long list of acknowledgments, Mrs. Dye expressed gratitude "to the Lewis and Clark families, especially to William Hancock Clark of Washington, D.C., and John O'Fallon Clark of St. Louis, grandsons of Governor Clark, and to C. Harper Anderson of Ivy Depot, Virginia, the nephew and heir of Meriwether Lewis, for letters, documents and family traditions." The list includes also "Reuben Gold Thwaites . . . for use of the original journals of Lewis and Clark, which Mr. Thwaites is now editing."

The Conquest begins in Virginia in the summer of 1774 when Meriwether Lewis was a tiny baby and William Clark was a charming red-head aged four. His oldest brother, George Rogers Clark, and their father were keenly aware of a probable war with England.

The story of the exploration of the West is told in Part II of *The Conquest.* Part III ends shortly after the death of former Governor Clark in St. Louis, in 1838, at the age of sixty-eight, when Indians "marched in the long funeral train of their Red Head Father and wept genuine tears of desolation." The final chapter tells how Patrick Gass, "honored everywhere as the last of the men of Lewis and Clark," died in his sleep in 1870 at the age of ninety-nine.

In Part II, Mrs. Dye gives tantalizing glimpses of several members of the Expedition. George Shannon is depicted as a handsome, jolly, singing boy of seventeen when he joined the Expedition. Sacagawea, "Madonna of the Expedition," appears from time to time, happy and useful. The chapter entitled "A Woman Pilot" is more accurate than the heading suggests, but the reader who knows the facts will be surprised by the fiction in the author's last statements about Sacagawea, in the chapter called "The Home Stretch." It was on August 17, 1806, according to Lewis and Clark, that "the principal chiefs of the Minnetarees came down to bid us farewell," and that the captains paid Charbonneau and said farewell to him and to Sacagawea.

Mrs. Dye romanticizes the scene thus:

All was now ready for the descent for St. Louis. The boats, lashed together in pairs, were at the shore. . . .
Sacajawea, modest princess of the Shoshones, heroine of the great

expedition, stood with her babe in arms and smiled upon them from the shore. So had she stood in the Rocky Mountains pointing out the gates. So had she followed the great rivers, navigating the continent.

Sacajawea's hair was neatly braided, her nose was fine and straight, and her skin pure copper like a statue in some Florentine gallery. Madonna of her race, she had led the way to a new time. To the hands of this girl, not yet eighteen, had been entrusted the key that unlocked the road to Asia.

Some day, upon the Bozeman Pass, Sacajawea's statue will stand beside that of Clark. Some day where the rivers part, her laurels will vie with those of Lewis. Across North America a Shoshone Indian princess touched hands with Jefferson, opening her country.

There is more fiction in the chapter that follows.

11

A Legend Begins: Sacagawea Becomes "the Guide"

TWO centennial expositions were held in the United States in the early years of the twentieth century, one of them in the Midwest and the other in the Far West. The Louisiana Purchase Exposition in St. Louis, planned for 1903, was actually held in 1904. The Lewis and Clark Centennial Exposition was held in Portland in 1905.

Sacagawea and Eva Emery Dye were important in each of them, partly because of the latter's historical novel *The Conquest*, and partly because of Mrs. Dye's intense interest in women's suffrage. In Clackamas County, where she lived, she was chairman of the Oregon Equal Suffrage Association. In fact, it seems to have been her keen interest in women's rights that led her to a study of Sacagawea. Her search for a heroine for *The Conquest* seems to suggest a good deal about her personality:

> I struggled along as best I could with the information I could get, trying to find a heroine. I traced down every old book and scrap of paper, but was still without a real heroine. Finally, I came upon the name of Sacajawea, and I screamed, 'I have found my heroine!'
> I then hunted up every fact I could find about Sacajawea. Out of a few dry bones I found in the old tales of the trip, I created Sacajawea and made her a living entity. For months I dug and scraped for accurate information about this wonderful Indian maid.

The world snatched at my heroine, Sacajawea . . . . The beauty of that faithful Indian woman with her baby on her back, leading those stalwart mountaineers and explorers through the strange land appealed to the world.

Not long after the publication of *The Conquest,* women of Portland organized the Sacajawea Statue Association and elected Mrs. Dye as its president. Soon she announced, with much pride, that St. Louis was planning "a monument for the Louisiana Purchase Exposition in honor of Sacajawea, the brave Shoshone princess who led the way across the continent." The sculptor Bruno Walter Zimm of New York had been commissioned to create a statue of Sacagawea for St. Louis. After some study of Shoshone culture, he felt ready to find the model for his statue, and he was advised to write to the Reverend John Roberts, who had been a missionary on the Wind River Reservation in Wyoming since 1883. Roberts suggested that Zimm consider Virginia Grant, whose home was on the Shoshone Reservation but who, at that time, was a student in the school for Indians in Carlisle, Pennsylvania. The sculptor visited the school and decided that the young Indian woman was "decidedly typical of this tribe." His search for a model aroused interest in Sacagawea and in the St. Louis Exposition. (Unfortunately, the statue that was created for the event seems to have disappeared.)

Mrs. Dye asked women's organizations throughout the United States to contribute to the cost of making another statue of Sacagawea for the Portland Lewis and Clark Exposition. Women in Oregon obtained part of their share by selling "Sacagawea buttons" and "Sacagawea spoons." Alice Cooper of Denver was the sculptor commissioned to create this statue for $7,000.

The National American Woman's Suffrage Association (the NAWSA) held its annual meeting in Portland in the summer of 1905. Women from every state were there for the dedication of the Cooper statue of Sacagawea, "the Indian woman who led the Lewis and Clark Expedition thousands of miles through the wilderness unknown to the white men" (*History of Woman Suffrage,* edited by Ida Husted Harper). The opening address was given by the most distinguished woman present: Susan B. Anthony, who had organized the National American Woman's Suffrage Association in 1860. Miss Anthony said, "This is the first time in history that a statue has been erected in memory of a woman who accomplished patriotic deeds. . . . This recognition of the assistance rendered by a woman in the discovery of this great section of the country is but the beginning of what is due. . . ."

After a brief address by the head of the Oregon Equal Suffrage Association, Eva Emery Dye presented the statue to the officials of the Lewis and Clark Centennial Exposition, an Indian boy sang "The Star Spangled Banner," and during "a tumult of applause. . . the flag floated away, revealing the idealized mother and her babe."

Thus the well-known statue of Sacagawea (with her right arm pointing westward!) was unveiled and dedicated. It was seen by about three million people who attended the Lewis and Clark Centennial Exposition. Handsome though the statue is, a close view of the face makes one wish that the sculptor had known that Sacagawea was a teen-aged mother, not a mature woman.

The tributes to the Indian girl spoken on Sacagawea Day in Portland seem less surprising than similar exaggerations in the address of Dr. Anna Howard Shaw, president of the NAWSA. "Dr. Shaw was so impressed with the responsibility of her office," wrote the editor of *History of Woman Suffrage,* "that for the first time she wrote her president's address and it was published in twelve columns of the *Women's Journal.*"

Here is most of her tribute to Sacagawea:

Others will speak of that brave band of immortals whose achievements your great Exposition commemorates, while we pay our tributes of honor and gratitude to the modest, unselfish, enduring little Shoshone squaw, who uncomplainingly trailed, canoed, climbed, slaved and starved with the men of the party, enduring all that they endured, with the addition of a helpless baby on her back. At a time in the weary march when the hearts of the leaders had well nigh fainted within them, when success or failure hung a mere chance in the balance, this woman came to their deliverance and pointed out to the captain the great Pass which led from the forks of the Three Rivers over the mountains.

Then silently strapping her papoose upon her back she led the way, interpreting and making friendly overtures to powerful tribes

of Indians, who but for her might at any moment have annihilated
that brave band of intrepid souls. . . .

Forerunner of civilization, great leader of men, patient and
motherly woman, we bow our hearts to do you honor! . . . May we
the daughters of an alien race. . .learn the lessons of calm endur-
ance, of patient persistence and unfaltering courage exemplified in
your life, in our efforts to lead men through the Pass of justice, which
goes over the mountains of prejudice and conservatism to the broad
land of the perfect freedom of a true republic; one in which men
and women together shall in perfect equality solve the problems of a
nation that knows no caste, no race, no sex in opportunity, in
responsibility or in justice! May 'the eternal womanly' ever lead us
on! . . ."

.And so Sacagawea, "the Guide of the Lewis and Clark
Expedition," began to walk, hand in hand, with women's
suffrage in Oregon in 1905. The real Sacagawea had been in
the Portland area in the fall of 1805 and in the spring of 1806,
but the speakers seem to have made no reference to that fact.
But Sacagawea was not "the guide" then: *the legend had not yet
been created.*

Probably many of the women attending this meeting of the
NAWSA had read one or both of these two magazine articles
recently published: "What the Portland Exposition Really
Celebrates," in the April 1905 issue of *The Review of Reviews*
and "Sacajawea, Bird Woman," in the June issue of *The
Woman's Home Companion. The Review of Reviews* was one of the
most widely read magazines of the day and the author of this
article, Agnes Laut, was well known for her books and her
writings on historical subjects. Here are a few excerpts from
her article:

The great difficulty . . . was to cross the Rockies—to go from
where the Missouri ended to where the Columbia began.

This was accomplished—not by the wisdom or the courage of the
leaders but by the quiet, unconscious heroism of one of the
burden-bearers—a simple, hard-working Indian woman, Sacajawea. . . . Sacajawea it was who piloted the explorers through the
fastnesses of the pathless mountains.

Among the illustrations with the article is a photograph of the
statue of Sacagawea in St. Louis, above which is the identifi-

cation: "Ideal portrait of the Squaw Sacajawea, who piloted the Lewis and Clark Expedition."

Agnes Laut had not done her home work, nor had Martha Cobb Sanford when she wrote "Sacajawea, the Bird Woman." Sanford's one-page article has this subtitle: "The story of the Indian Heroine Who Just a Century Ago Found the Path for Lewis and Clark in Their Expedition to the Pacific. This article is Especially Timely as the Lewis and Clark Exposition Opens at Portland, Oregon, this Month." The author did quote correctly ten lines from the Biddle–Coues *History of the Expedition*, but much of the short article was from the author's imagination. Some typical phrases are quoted here:

And so early in November, she [Sacagawea] visited Captains Lewis and Clark . . . and offered her services as guide, which was accepted. Her husband had already been engaged as interpreter. The Frenchman and his captive girl-wife now joined the camp of the white men.

At length the little fleet reached "Sunday Island" and a creek, to which they gave the name "Chabonneau" [*sic*]. Beyond the latter point not a man among them had ever ventured. For the rest of the way they must rely upon their intuition and the guidance of the Indian woman.

She knew, also, how to cure rattlesnake bites by making a medicine from herbs. Finally Sacjawea herself fell ill with a fever, and since the party was dependent upon her for guidance, it was necessary to call a halt for several weeks.

True to her promise to guide the white men over the mountains, she begged help of her brother Cameawait, the chief, telling him of the white men's kindness to her, especially during her illness.

In 1907, readers interested in the history of the United States had a new opportunity to learn about it—in the first issue of the *Journal of American History*. In the September issue of the new quarterly was an article with this title and subtitle: "Pilot of First White Men to Cross the American Continent: Identification of the Indian Girl who led the Lewis and Clark Expedition over the Rocky Mountains in their Unparalleled Journey into the Mysteries of the Western World—Recognition of Sacajawea as the Woman Who Guided the Explorers to the New Golden Empire." The author was Grace Raymond

Hebard, Ph.D., of the faculty of the University of Wyoming. Here are some excerpts:

The most hazardous and the most significant journey ever made on the Western Continent, a journey that rivals in daring and exceeds in importance the expeditions of Stanley and Livingston in the wilds of Africa—a journey. . . that gave to the world riches beyond comprehension—was piloted by a woman. . . .

Charbonneau received from Lewis and Clark for his services the sum of five hundred dollars and a few odd cents. There is no record to show that Sacajawea received any compensation by gift or word. It is true we find the following in the 'Journals': 'This man [Charbonneau] has been very serviceable to us, and his wife particularly useful among the Shoshones. Indeed, she has borne with a patience truly admirable the fatigues of so long a route, encumbered with the charge of an infant, who is even now only nineteen months old . . .'

Suddenly, the rhythm changes. The two sentences just quoted are easily found in Coues, in the first paragraph dated August 17, 1806. But the next five sentences that Miss Hebard includes in her supposed quotation are not in Coues, nor in the Thwaites edition of the journals, nor in the letter that Clark wrote to Charbonneau in the pirogue on August 20, 1806. Here is the remainder of the paragraph that Miss Hebard pretends to quote from the journals:

She [Sacagawea] was very observant. She had a good memory, remembering locations not seen since her childhood. In trouble she was full of resources, plucky and determined. With her helpless infant she rode with the men, guiding us unerringly through mountain passes and lonely places. Intelligent, cheerful, resourceful, tireless, faithful, she inspired us all.

Women were not the only contributors to the legend of "Sacagawea, the Guide." George Creel glorified her in an article written for *Colliers, the American Weekly* in 1926. It was one of a series of articles he wrote "on great figures of the romantic past." Creel had been editor of three newspapers in the West and was the author of at least four books on historical subjects. Here is the second paragraph in his article about the Lewis and Clark Expedition:

Few historians sing the glory of this obscure Indian girl, yet with a two-months old baby at her breast, she led Lewis and Clark up the wild reaches of the Missouri and over saw-toothed ranges; when the white captains wandered hopelessly amid enormities of granite, her unerring instinct found a way; when hostile Indians gathered to dispute the march of the staggering band, it was Sacajawea that trudged forward, holding her papoose high in token of peace and friendship; at a time when starvation threatened, she took from her tattered buckskin the store of food she had saved from her own pitiful ration.

Later in the article, Creel says: "and as the Expedition reached the Bitterroot Valley—staggering with exhaustion— it was Sacajawea that gained the friendship of the Flatheads." Still later, "Nez Perces were camped in the pleasant Kamas prairie and soft-voiced Sacajawea convinced them that the white men came as friends."

In George W. Fuller's *A History of the Pacific Northwest* (revised edition of 1938), she is identified as "Sacajawea, who became famous as the principal guide of the expedition." Fuller's volume, for several years, was a textbook in colleges and universities in the Northwest.

In an encyclopedia used chiefly by young readers, Sacagawea was "the principal guide" of the expedition until a new edition was published in 1973. In biographies of Sacagawea written for children, she has been "the guide," sometimes in the title.

And in many newspapers, she has been called "the guide"— at least through the summer of 1976. In that year, the State of Montana celebrated the national bicentennial with a three-day festival and the dedication of three newly sculptured figures at Fort Benton. There, Lewis and Clark, erect and handsome, stand on a rock; beside them sits youthful Sacagawea with her baby on her back. Newspapers in the area published a photograph of the unusual sculpture and, in their comments below it, identified the young Indian woman as "the guide of the expedition."

Probably Grace Hebard's article would have reached only the few readers of the new historical journal if it had not been reprinted in one of the two books by James Schultz published in 1918. The book has the title *Bird Woman (Sacajawea), the Guide of Lewis and Clark: Her Own Story Now Given to the World.* "Away back in the 1870's," Schultz says in the first paragraph of this book, "I went from New York to Fort Benton, Montana, to see something of the buffalo country." He lived among the Blackfeet for more than thirty years, and Indians from several tribes became his good friends. He greatly enjoyed the stories told around the winter fires and, using them, he became the author of several "Westerns." Among the stories he heard "were tales about Sacajawea, the heroine— yes, the savior—of the Lewis and Clark Expedition."

Many years later, when there seemed to be a keen interest in the subject, he decided to write the story as it had been related to him, he claimed, by three old friends of Sacagawea: a Mandan woman, an Arikara woman, and a white man. Schultz told it in the first person, as if Sacagawea were really speaking. It ends with the departure of the explorers down the Missouri in August 1806, "and then I went off by myself and cried." Today, the book seems like historical fiction, but in 1918 it was praised as biography in at least two respected magazines. And in at least some libraries today, it is still classified as biography.

Bird Woman became a popular book. Valuable to uninformed readers is an Appendix, which quotes most references to Sacagawea in the Coues edition, except those in the footnotes. Schultz's Appendix begins with Captain Clark's statement of November 11, 1804 about the visit of the two Shoshone wives of Charbonneau. It ends with an *accurate* copy of the statements about Sacagawea in the entry of August 17, 1806. But in the chapter "The Rest of Her Story," Schultz includes Hebard's fabrication.

Hebard's article in the *Journal of American History* in 1907 was neither her last nor her most important effort to convince the reading public that Sacagawea was "the guide" of the Lewis and Clark Expedition. She conducted long interviews with several elderly Shoshones on the Wind River Reservation and did much other research for her book, as her bibliography indicates. At last it was published in 1932, with this title: *Sacajawea: A guide and interpreter of the Lewis and Clark expedition, with an account of the travels of Toussaint Charbonneau, and of Jean Baptiste, the expedition papoose.*

Integrity is a quality naturally expected of a person in Professor Hebard's important position. But frequently in her book she referred to Sacagawea as "the guide"—three times in two consecutive pages. And she carefully prepared for the appearance of the "Guide" on the last page of her book. Much of the forty-five pages of her chapter "With the Lewis and Clark Expedition" consists of quotations from the Biddle edition of the journals. But she reduced 7,300 words to about 225 concerning the search for the Shoshones that Captain Lewis and three men made between August 9 and 17, 1805. (See Chapter 3 above for this story.) More than half of what Hebard wrote about the search is the incident on August 11 when "Captain Lewis perceived, with the greatest delight, an Indian on horseback, and was unsuccessful in making the sign of friendship customary with the Missouri River and Rocky Mountain Indians." Her only statement suggesting the purpose of the journey is not entirely correct: "and after much bickering and bartering he [Chief Cameahwait] agreed to furnish horses and a guide to pilot the expedition over the mountains." In fact, there was no "bickering or bartering." It did take time for Lewis to persuade Chief Cameahwait and a few of his men to accompany the white men eastward over the mountains to meet Captain Clark and the main party, but he succeeded, and then he recorded, for President Jefferson, a great deal of valuable information about the personality and the life of the Shoshone nation.

Hebard carefully prepared a surprise for the ending of her biography. Her seventh appendix lists "Sacajawea Memorials," the last of which is a reserve formally dedicated to the Indian girl as "the Montana and Idaho Interstate Sacajawea national monument." This is her chief sentence about it:

> The preserve is situated at Lemhi pass on the summit of 7500 feet of the continental divide at the boundary between Montana and Idaho, where in August, 1805, Sacajawea guided the explorers over the Rocky Mountains to the west.

Suddenly, the alert reader understands why Hebard mentioned no mountains when she gave her very brief account of the journey of Captain Lewis and his three men in search of the Shoshones and their horses. According to the journals, on August 12, 1805, they had walked west on an Indian road that passed through a "small gap formed by the high mountains."

(That "gap" has long been known as Lemhi Pass.) When Lewis and his three men returned eastward, they were accompanied by Chief Cameahwait and a few Shoshones.

Two days later, Chief Cameahwait and all his people with him except two men and two women, started westward, accompanied by Sacagawea and Charbonneau. In a short time, Sacagawea and her husband returned eastward over the Continental Divide and through the gap (Lemhi Pass), with Chief Cameahwait, about fifty men (with their women and children), and the horses they were willing to sell to the explorers.

Early in the morning of August 26, Captain Lewis and all of the explorers who were not with Captain Clark started westward again with Chief Cameahwait and several Shoshones, both men and women. Soon they crossed the "dividing ridge." They had traveled through Lemhi Pass and had crossed the Continental Divide. Obviously, on the fifth trip through Lemhi Pass, *no guide was needed!*

Thus we have seen that the legend about the "guide of the Lewis and Clark Expedition" was *created* by (1) Eva Emery Dye, historical novelist of the Northwest and a county chairman of the Oregon Equal Suffrage Association; (2) Dr. Anna Howard Shaw, a graduate of Boston University Medical School and president of the National Woman Suffrage Association from 1904–1915; and (3) Dr. Grace Hebard, Librarian and Professor at the University of Wyoming for many years.

Equally responsible for expounding the legend were: George Creel in *Collier's American Weekly,* George W. Fuller in *A History of the Pacific Northwest* (1938), *Collier's Encyclopedia,* Portland *Oregonian* and *Journal* (June 28, 1905), National American Woman's Suffrage Association, and Susan B. Anthony.

12

Sacagawea, a Controversial Figure

IN her article in the *Journal of American History* of 1907, Hebard is chiefly concerned with her belief that Sacagawea lived on the Wind River Reservation, in western Wyoming, in her old age and died there in 1884. Apparently, Hebard was the first person who had ever expressed that idea in print. Her invention of a supposed quotation from Lewis's and Clark's journals published in the article of 1907 calling Sacagawea "the guide" makes one question her other assumptions. Before we consider them, we need to know certain facts.

On March 3, 1807, Congress passed "an act making compensation to Messrs. Lewis and Clarke [sic] and their companions." Each captain received 1,600 acres of land. Each of thirty-one men whose names were listed (including "heirs and legal representatives of Charles Floyd deceased") received 320 acres. "Tousaint Charbono" was on the list but Sacagawea's name does not appear.

According to Hidatsa tradition, a year or so after the return of the Expedition, some fur traders came from up the river and stayed with the Hidatsas in North Dakota for a few days. When they started down the river for St. Louis, they took with them Charbonneau and his two Shoshone wives with their children.

Later, Charbonneau decided to try farming, perhaps influenced by Captain Clark's suggestion in his letter. According to a contract signed October 30, 1810, he bought some
land from Clark along the Missouri River, not far from
St. Louis. Clark was then Superintendent of Indian Affairs in
the Louisiana Territory (soon changed to Missouri Territory). But in a few months, Charbonneau sold the tract of
land back to Clark for $100. He had decided to return to fur
trading and to life with the Indians on the plains. He
purchased fifty pounds of "biscuit" or "hard tack," apparently
preparing for a long journey.

That Charbonneau took only one of his wives with him we
know from the journal of Henry Brackenridge, a lawyer and
future author, who came from Pittsburgh and kept a journal
for a book about his travels. Brackenridge had tried to
practice law in Pennsylvania but decided that there were
probably greater opportunities in the West, and he spent the
years 1810 to 1814 in Missouri and Louisiana, practicing law
and getting acquainted with his surroundings. In March
1811, he made a voyage up the Missouri River with Manuel
Lisa, who was important in the Missouri Fur Company. Here
is a paragraph from Brackenridge's journal:

> We have on board a Frenchman named Charbonet, with his wife,
> an Indian woman of the Snake nation, both of whom accompanied
> Lewis and Clark to the Pacific, and were of great service. The
> woman, a good creature of mild and gentle disposition, was greatly
> attached to the whites, whose manners and aims she tried to imitate;
> but she had become sickly and longed to revisit her native country;
> her husband also, who had spent many years amongst the Indians,
> was become weary of a civilized life.

We know that the wife was not on her way to "her native
country," but can we accept the idea that she had been in the
exploring party? Did Brackenridge know that Charbonneau
had two "Snake" or Shoshone wives? Perhaps this was the
one called Otter Woman by the Minnetarees but not named
in Clark's brief mention on November 11, 1804. Otter Woman was said, by the Hidatsa or Minnetaree historian, Chief
Poor Wolf, to have been unwell when the explorers were near
the Mandans. And it is hard to believe that Sacagawea had

become "sickly" in the short time since her vigorous life with the Expedition.

Being interested in the Far West, Brackenridge may have read Sergeant Gass's journal. It was the first of the explorers' journals to be published and was very popular at the time. In the absorbing story of the exploration, it would be possible to forget Gass's brief mention that "three squaws, wives to our interpreter," silently watched the white men's Christmas dance in 1804 and his brief statement in February 1805 about the birth of a baby to "one of our interpreter's wives." And of course Brackenridge may not have seen Gass's book until after his own journal was published. In 1814, remember, even Governor Clark had difficulties getting a copy of the *History of the Expedition.*

Charbonneau was surely aware that Manuel Lisa was on the boat and that if he was to return to the fur business, he would want to make a favorable impression on him. He probably did not know whether that important fur trader had become accustomed to "squaw men," as white men with Indian wives came to be called. Charbonneau joined the Lisa expedition in 1812, the year following the trip up the river with Brackenridge. The party went in search of furs to be purchased from hunters, both Indians and white men.

Surely if either of Charbonneau's sons had been on the boat in 1811, Brackenridge would have mentioned him. It seems logical to conclude that both boys were left in or near St. Louis in charge of Sacagawea. Jean Baptiste had had his sixth birthday the preceding month, and Toussaint, Jr., was about eight. The Sacagawea that we know would certainly be capable of taking care of them. Among the Indians, a woman was considered the mother not only of her own children, but also of her step-children, nieces, and nephews.

The next known reference to a wife of Charbonneau was written in December 1812 by John Luttig, but did not become known until his journal was published in 1920. Luttig had been a merchant in Baltimore before he came to St. Louis. From August 1812 until the spring of 1813, "he served as clerk of the Missouri Fur Company on its expedition up the Missouri."

The first entry in Luttig's journal begins: "Friday the 8th of May I started from St. Louis . . ." His last five entries were written during the first five days of March, 1813. On December 20, 1812, he wrote his best-known entry: "this evening the Wife of Charbonneau a Snake Squaw, died of a putrid fever she was a good and the best woman in the fort, aged abt 25 years she left a fine infant girl." It is unfortunate for us that Luttig did not identify the woman by name. Perhaps he did not know it. Notice that he wrote "the wife of Charbonneau," not "a wife." Very likely he did not know that the Frenchman had two Shoshone wives. Like Brackenridge, Luttig was rather new in the West.

Notice also that the year was 1812. War between the British and the United States had been brewing for several years, especially along the upper Mississippi River. There, several Indian tribes fought on the side of the British after war was declared in June 1812. In March 1813, British and Indians attacked Fort Manuel, named for Manuel Lisa and built on the bank of the Missouri River in what is now South Dakota, and it had to be abandoned.

Charbonneau was away on fur-trading business, and so, in June 1813, kind-hearted John Luttig took the baby Lizette with him to St. Louis. Believing that the father was dead and finding that Governor Clark was away, Luttig applied at the Orphan's Court for the adoption of Charbonneau's children. When Governor Clark returned, Luttig's name was crossed out and William Clark was written above it. This record is dated August 11, 1813:

William Clark

The court appoints ~~John Luttig~~ guardian to the infant children of Tousant Charbonneau deceased, to wit Tousant Charbonneau, a boy about the age of ten years, and Lizette Charbonneau a girl about one year old. The said Indian children, not being possessed of any property within the knowledge of the court, the said guardian is not required to give bond.

In 1920, Luttig's journal, containing his report of the death of "the wife of Charbonneau" was published by the Missouri Historical Society with the title *Journal of a Fur-Trading Expedition on the Upper Missouri 1812–1813*, by John C. Luttig,

Clerk of the Missouri Fur Company. Stella Drumm, Librarian of the Missouri Historical Society edited it. In the collections there, she had discovered the unsigned manuscript in the Society's collection and later found the name of the author and some facts about him. The Appendix contains a few letters relative to Luttig or Charbonneau, biographical sketches of "Sakakawea," Charbonneau, and Manuel Lisa, and then shorter sketches of eleven other men of the period.

A footnote to Luttig's entry of December 20, 1812 leads to Miss Drumm's biographical sketch of "Sakakawea." She preferred that spelling because it was used by Dr. Washington Matthews, "a recognized authority on the ethnology and philology of the Hidatsa." Drumm's biographical résumé of Sacagawea contains this puzzling sentence: "Charbonneau probably had two Snake wives, as 'two squaw prisoners from the Rock Mountains and purchased by Charbonneau', visited the winter camp of Lewis and Clark at the Mandan village. One, of course, was the Bird Woman, and James Schultz says that the name of the other was Otter Woman and that she died shortly after the return of the expedition." When Schultz's book was published in 1918, 1812 naturally seemed a short time after 1806.

In a later paragraph Miss Drumm said, "Several times, we are informed by the journals of Lewis and Clark, Sakakawea was dangerously ill. It is not likely that the hardships of this frail child-woman endured following her capture, and again on that long journey to the Far West, shortened her life."

We cannot accept this speculation. Only two illnesses of Sacagawea were reported in the Journals. The second one was of little consequence and was shared with several men— sea-sickness—on November 8 near the mouth of the Columbia River, when the swells were so high that the canoes rolled. The first and only serious illness began June 10, 1805, and is described in Chapter 2 of this book. On June 24, Captain Lewis reported "The Indian woman is perfectly recovered."

What did Sacagawea do five days later? With a little assistance from Captain Clark, she climbed up a steep and rocky hill above a river. Also remember that she was carrying her baby in her arms and that during a part of the struggle

uphill, they were in "a torrent of rain and hail." Sacagawea
was so wet and cold that Clark hurried the group to camp. He
was "fearful of a relapse," but none was reported.

Both leaders and several men were ill in September when
they were with the Nez Perces, after their dangerous horseback ride over the Rockies and after "the free use of food to
which [they] had not been accustomed." Evidently Sacagawea
was not ill. In January 1806, that strenuous trip to see the
whale was not taken by a "frail child-woman," nor was the
horseback trip in the spring, eastward, over the snow-covered
Rocky Mountains.

A second reason for not accepting Drumm's biographical
sketch of "Sakakawea" as completely factual is based upon
Clark's letter to Charbonneau written in the pirogue on
August 20, 1806, on the way to St. Louis. These are his exact
words and his spelling:

> your little son (my boy Pomp), . . . your son Baptiest, . . . If you are
> desposed to accept either of my offers to you and you will bring
> down your *Son* your famn [wife] Janey had best come along with you
> to take care of the boy until I get him.

And now read his farewell to Charbonneau, not included in
Chapter 11:

> Wishing you and your family great suckcess & with anxious expecta-
> tion of seeing my dancing boy Baptiest I shall remain your friend,
>   William Clark

It is noteworthy that in the journals of Lewis and Clark, all
references to the baby seem to be to "the Child," except for
one reference to "Charbono's son." Probably "Pomp" was
recognized when Clark named "Pompey's Pillar."

A footnote to "my boy Pomp" in Donald Jackson's copy of
this letter in his volume concerning Lewis and Clark leads to
this information: "Jean Baptiste Charbonneau, born 11 Feb.
1805 at Fort Mandan." When one considers that this fact is
found in many authoritative sources, it is astonishing to read
that Miss Drumm did not realize that the two names refer to
the same child! She wrote:

> In Gov. Clark's letter of August 20, 1806, he clearly mentions two
> boys, children of Charbonneau. One he refers to as 'your little son

(my boy Pomp)' and the other he calls 'my little dancing boy Baptiest.' The dancing boy was too old to be the child of Sakakawea whose birthday has been established.

Apparently Drumm believed that a nineteen−months old child could not be a "dancing boy."

Miss Drumm went on to say that "Jean Baptiste Charbonneau was most likely the Baptiste mentioned in Clark's letter and the son of one of his other wives, who with her child was at the Mandan Fort in the winter of 1804−1805." But she gave no source of her statement; it is not found in the journals of the explorers edited by Thwaites.

When John Luttig applied in the Orphan's Court in St. Louis for "Toussant Charbonneau, a boy about the age of ten years," Jean Baptiste Charbonneau, son of Sacagawea, was exactly eight years and four months old. Surely the deceased mother was the other Shoshone wife of Charbonneau. That Luttig did not know about her is apparent from his having written in his journal "the wife of Charbonneau"— not "a wife."

In spite of the fact that Miss Drumm was an historian, she gave no convincing evidence that Sacagawea was "the wife of Charbonneau," who died December 20, 1812. Apparently Drumm did not visualize the young mother's two journeys over the Rocky Mountains in the cold and the snow. Apparently she did not visualize the voluntary and difficult journey, chiefly on foot, to see the whale. Drumm must have forgotten the hundreds of miles the explorers traveled eastward, chiefly on foot and horseback. Sacagawea really showed amazing vigor again and again.

The publication of Luttig's journal caused some confusion. The many readers of James Schultz's biography of Sacagawea had learned from his quotation from the elderly missionary on the Wind River Reservation that she had been buried by him in the Shoshone cemetery in April 1884. Schultz had quoted both the missionary and Hebard's article—only two years before the publication of Luttig's journal.

Bird Woman revived the interest in Sacagawea that had been aroused by the centennial celebrations, by the statues of the Indian woman, and by the articles and books about her—so much interest that the Bureau of Indian Affairs decided to have a monument placed at her grave. So in 1924, the Commissioner of Indian Affairs asked the distinguished Indian, Dr. Charles Eastman, to do some research, in order to locate "the final resting place of Sacajawea or Bird Woman."

Eastman was a Sioux, whose Indian name was *Ohiyesa,* pronounced "O-hee-ya-sah." He did not see a white person until he was sixteen years old. He graduated from Dartmouth College in 1887 and from the School of Medicine of Boston University in 1891. When he was asked to make the investigation, he had written nine books, all about Indians.

Clearly, Eastman was well qualified to make the investigation, and on each reservation he had the cooperation of the government officials, including the interpreter. He felt handicapped, however, as soon as he learned that Sacagawea had done a good deal of wandering. He was expected to complete the investigation in two months—January and February 1925. He spent most of his time on the Wind River Reservation, where several people had known Sacagawea, "Basil's Mother," all of her years there. He also went to North Dakota for information from the Indians called Minnetarees by Lewis and Clark, and to Oklahoma to interview Comanches.

Eastman knew that a tribal historian was carefully trained by his elders. One who wished to become the tribal historian heard the factual traditions related over and over by the tribal historian, and then the youth himself related the historic traditions in the presence of his elders, evening after evening, until they were correct. As the Indians had no written language, they preserved their history and their literature by storytelling. Both the factual stories and the imaginative tales made good entertainment around the winter fires.

When Doctor Eastman learned that Sacagawea, a Shoshone Indian, had lived among the Hidatsas, he went to Fort Berthold, North Dakota. There he was fortunate in having interviews with Mrs. Weidemann, the daughter of Chief Poor Wolf and "a very intelligent woman." She spoke not only Hidatsa, but also English and Sioux. They conversed in the Sioux language.

Poor Wolf was not only chief during much of the nineteenth century, but also tribal historian. He was a boy when the Lewis and Clark Expedition spent the winter near the Hidatsas. He lived until 1902 and had "a very clear mind until his death." His daughter, aged eighty in 1925, had heard him tell the tribal traditions for so many years that she still knew them. We have given her story earlier in Chapter 2 (p. 14).

In his report to the Commissioner of Indian Affairs, Eastman summarized this interview with Mrs. Weidemann in one long paragraph:

> This evidence given by Wolf Chief of the Hidatsas and by Mrs. Weidemann shows that Charbonneau did have two Shoshone wives. . . . They clearly stated that Charbonneau took both of his Shoshone wives with him when he visited St. Louis some time in 1807 to 1808. . . . [He went to that region to gather furs to be sold at home and abroad. Beaver clothing—including beaver hats with beaver tails—had wide popularity.]
>
> It is evident that he returned with but one Shoshone wife, who died on December 20, 1812. In the St. Louis court application for the guardians of his children, the child of Bird Woman was conspicuously absent. It will seem, then, that this child had been left in St. Louis when Charbonneau returned north in 1811 but the child Baptiste would have been too young to have been separated from his mother, the Bird Woman.

Elsewhere in his report, Eastman gives a little more information about his final statement just quoted:

> . . . to my knowledge, the Indian mother's traits and habits are such that she could not have permitted (herself) to be separated from her child of that age, especially in those times. It was hard enough up to thirty years ago to get a child of 10 years to go to school.

In 1962, a very brief record of the death of Sacagawea, written by William Clark between 1825–1828, appeared in print for the first time. A 700-page volume with the title *Letters of the Lewis and Clark Expedition with Related Documents 1783–1854* was published by the University of Illinois Press. The researcher, a very thorough one, and editor was Donald Jackson.[12] On pages 638–639 is "Clark's List of Expedition Members. This document appears on the front cover of

Clark's cash book and journal for 1825–1828, and seems according to internal evidence, to have been written during those years." Beside most of the thirty-four names on the list is some brief notation, such as "Dead" beside "Se car ja we uh."[13]

There can be little doubt that John Luttig was Governor Clark's informant about the death of "the wife of Charbonneau," when he brought the infant Lizette with him to St. Louis in the spring of 1813. Luttig's report of the death of "the wife of Charbonneau," wrote John Bakeless, "would fix the date of Sacagawea's death—except that Charbonneau had two Shoshone wives." We recall that the second wife was mentioned only once in the explorers' journals and that Clark did not mention her in his letter to Charbonneau.

13

Some of Eastman's Discoveries

DR. Charles Eastman recorded another story from Mrs. Weidemann about Sacagawea. When Chief Poor Wolf was about twenty-one years old (circa 1820), Charbonneau took a Hidatsa girl named Eagle as his wife. A year or so later, he took Eagle with him down the river with some fur traders. She was gone eleven or twelve years, and when she returned, strange to say, she came from up the river. Eagle told Mrs. Weidemann's father all about her trip. "He repeated her story so many times to his family and to the tribe," said Mrs. Weidemann, "that I still remember the substance of it." She told it in the first person, as if Eagle were speaking, and in much more detail than it will be given here:

When Charbonneau took Eagle down the river among the white people, they came to a great town called St. Louis. After they had been there a year or so, "Charbonneau found one of his Shoshone wives—'the Bird Woman'—Sacajawea." She was living in a little town up the river from St. Louis. She had two sons with her: Bazil, who was about eighteen, and Baptiste, who was about fifteen, Eagle thought. They were bright young men and spoke French quite well. Sacagawea also spoke the language.

After a while, Charbonneau wanted to take Sacagawea as his wife again, and Eagle consented. So they all lived together for a time in St. Louis. Charbonneau was working for the

Missouri Fur Company. Then they were sent down a large river, almost as big as the Missouri River. On this trip they came to a great many trading posts. They stopped at one place for a year and at another place for two years.

They came among many Indian tribes that Eagle had never heard of. Some were called Wichitas, some Comanches, some Utes. Other tribes came to the trading posts where they were staying. After a while, Charbonneau took another wife, a pretty and young Ute woman. Eagle did not mind, but Bird Woman complained so much that she made life unpleasant for the Ute girl. Finally, Charbonneau whipped Sacagawea severely. A day or two afterward, she disappeared.

At this time Bazil and Baptiste were away on a trip to other bands of Indians to get furs. When they returned and learned what Charbonneau had done, they were never friends again with their father, and they did not see their mother for many years.

The following summer, the Fur Company organized a large number of their employees for a long trip. With many packed mules they traveled to the mountain Indians toward the Northwest. Charbonneau, Eagle, and the Ute woman joined the party. They traveled a long distance until they came to a big lake. White people called it Salt Lake.

There they stayed all winter. Many of the men trapped beaver along the streams of the mountains and bought furs from the Indians. In the summer, Charbonneau and his two wives were to move northeast over the mountains, but before they started, some relatives of Charbonneau's Ute wife visited their winter quarters. The wife went home with her relatives and Charbonneau and Eagle never saw her again. They traveled down three rivers until they reached the Missouri and then down the Missouri until they reached what Eagle considered her home in a Hidatsa village.

"This is all that I can remember" was Mrs. Weidemann's ending.

The remainder of Charbonneau's wives (seemingly all of them young) do not belong in this story. His last appearance in print was in 1839. Then eighty years old and feeble, he tottered into the Office of Indian Affairs in St. Louis, to ask for his salary as interpreter among the Mandans. Smallpox had almost wiped out the Mandans in 1837, but the superintendent thought the old man should be paid. The time and place of his death are not known.

How much wandering Sacagawea did before she lived among the Comanche Indians in Oklahoma is not known. The Comanches and the Shoshones are closely related and speak almost the same language. One of Sacagawea's great-grandsons, James McAdams, said that he "used to get her to talk Comanche because it sounded funny."

McAdams seemingly was not on the Wind River Reservation when Eastman made his investigation. Such a well-informed relative of Sacagawea surely was not overlooked. Four years later, he gave a long testimony to Grace Hebard, certified (as were the testimonies to Eastman) by the official interpreter on the reservation. McAdams had lived with his grandfather Bazil and his great-grandmother Sacagawea "four or five or more years," from the age of six until he went to the new school for Indians at Carlisle, Pennsylvania in 1881. She died while he was there. He remembered her as "a good-natured woman, always jolly."

He had seen many times the medal that she or one of her sons wore on special occasions and he remembered clearly the small leather wallet in which she carried some papers "so as to show she was worth something." After Sacagawea's death, Bazil carried the papers until his death. McAdams said that she told him often about going with "soldiers away off into the country clear to the big waters in the west." Like others on the reservation, McAdams remembered her tell of the time when the soldiers were starving, and how they had killed a horse for meat.

His great-grandmother told him a little about her French husband. He was rough in his treatment of her, she said, and "she ran away from him after he had whipped her." She told the boy several times that she had relatives in Oklahoma. "You have relatives," she told him, "down in the south with the Comanches. I left a son there with them, whose name was Ticannaf."

Soon after McAdams became a student at Carlisle, he made the acquaintance of the Comanche boys.

"Do you know anything about my Grandmother Porivo or Sacajawea?" he asked them. (Porivo means "Chief.")

Eventually McAdams learned that a granddaughter and some other descendants of Porivo still lived in Oklahoma. After a while, the two families visited with each other. They considered themselves brothers and sisters, not cousins.

When Eastman visited the Comanches, he had interviews with three women who had clear recollections of Porivo. One of them was her granddaughter, who was about ninety years old. Naturally she was more informative than the others.

"My name is Tacutine," she told Eastman through an interpreter, "and I am the daughter of Ticannaf, son of Porivo. The story of my grandmother is told in this way":

She married Jerk-Meat and had five children. [Eastman reported that three of them died in infancy.] My father was her second son. Soon after my father had two children, my grandmother disappeared. My grandfather Jerk-Meat had been killed in battle, and my grandmother was very unhappy. For some reason she had trouble with the people around her, and she said that she wouldn't live with the Comanches any more. People thought that she did not mean it.

But one morning she departed, nobody knows where. She took her daughter with her, and carried some dried buffalo meat in a leather bag. The people worried about her and hunted all over for her for a long time. Some even went to other tribes, to see if she had gone there. But nothing had been heard of her. We all thought that she had been killed or [had] perished somewhere.

After we were put on reservations, some Comanche boys went to Carlisle School. There a Comanche boy named Howard met a boy by the name of McAdams, a Shoshone from Fort Washakie, Wyoming. This boy, McAdams, asked Howard if there were any relatives of Porivo living among the Comanches. Howard told him he thought that there were.

When Howard came home from school, I learned all that McAdams had told him about Porivo, my grandmother, being on the Wind River Reservation and dying there. We could hardly believe it, but McAdams knew the names of Porivo's children who lived here on this reservation. So we knew that she must have been my grandmother.

Since then, by correspondence, we became acquainted with her grandchildren on the Wind River Reservation. I visited them once or twice, and her grandson, Andrew Bazil, visited us here once. And some of her great-grandchildren, the McAdamses, have been here quite often.

We never knew that my grandmother had been married before she married my grandfather here, and we never knew that she had any children anywhere but here. The story is well known now among the Comanches that she had traveled with some white people to the Shoshone country. . . .

We never knew that my grandmother had married a white man by the name of Charbonneau or that she had traveled with some soldiers across the Rocky Mountains to the sea. And we never suspected that she had been among any other tribe of Indians before she married my grandfather, Jerk-Meat.

Two other Comanche women told Eastman a similar story. One added the fact that Porivo died at "a very advanced age." One said that Porivo had had two sons on the Wind River Reservation, but that they had died. All but two of her [Porivo's] grandchildren there had died. One of Eastman's informants said, "It must be fully 70 years or more ago when Porivo disappeared from here."

Among the Comanches, after her disappearance, Sacagawea was usually called Wadze-wipe, meaning Lost Woman. Not one of the three informants said anything about the daughter she took with her. On the Wind River Reservation, one of the Shoshones who mentioned Sacagawea's life among the Comanches said that she had lived with them "a long time." It was obviously long enough for her second son to marry and to have two children. Two Comanches thought that she had lived with them for twenty-five or twenty-six years.

If it really was seventy years before 1925 that Sacagawea left the Comanches, she left them about 1855. What did she do during the years before she is known to have been with her people?

Eastman gathered almost no information about that period of her life. In this letter to the Commissioner, he spoke of the short time that he was given for his investigation. Consequently, it was difficult for him "to go into all the trails and evidences of her wanderings." He went only to the important points where she actually lived.

Several of his informants on the Wind River Reservation

reported that they had first seen her, in their childhood, at a meeting at Fort Bridger that is known to have been held in 1868.

But even the relatives that she had lived with said that she had talked little about her life with the Comanches. And her neighbor Finn Burnett said that if she had ever told him that she had a Comanche husband, he had forgotten. It is not surprising that she did not talk about her later years. It is very common among elderly people to remember their youth more clearly and more often than their later years.

The known facts about Sacagawea between her leaving the Comanches and her reunion with the Shoshones are fragmentary. But in his old age, Tom Rivington, then living in Nebraska, seemed to recall clearly Sacagawea's wandering when he was a boy. He wrote his recollections of her in letters to Hebard. He had known Sacagawea in 1860–1862, when she was living, part of the time, among the Indians near Virginia City, Montana. Just a boy, he "slept in her tent many times" and ran errands for her.

"She was a woman that was not satisfied anywhere," he wrote, "and the stage companies helped to make her this way, for they gave her free rides." Jack Slade, road agent for the stage company in Montana, Wyoming, and Colorado, gave "orders to let her eat at the stage stations, and ride on the stage free of all charges whenever she wanted to."

Sacagawea told the boy, Tom Rivington, that she had lived with different tribes in Canada, with the Apaches in Arizona, and with some tribes in California. The Apaches were always at war, she said, because "the whites made them that way." The California Indians "were poor, as the whites had taken all their land from them." According to Nez Perce tradition reported by John Bakeless, she lived for a long time with the Nez Perces in the Northwest. Rivington reported the same tradition.

Was Sacagawea a wanderer by nature, or had the experiences of her youth given her the desire to travel? Or was she trying to forget her grief caused by her second husband's death? "She was much devoted to him," wrote Eastman.

"Therefore, at his death she was heart-broken and much depressed."

Did she hesitate to return to her people because she had helped bring the whites to the region and other whites were now taking the land from the Indians? Did she travel because she was lonely, without family and without her people? Or did she travel because of intelligent curiosity, like Prince Paul of Würtemberg?

She visited the Blackfeet Indians more than once, wrote Rivington, and sometimes she lived with the Bannock Indians at Fort Hall in what is now southern Idaho. "The white people in those days had a worship for her. She did not have to pay for anything at the store for they gave her these things."

In 1862 Rivington went with her to visit some Bannocks again. Before they started, the owner or manager of the stages gave her ten dollars, as well as the usual free ride. From the Bannocks, they went to Fort Laramie, about eighty miles northeast in what is now the present city of Laramie, Wyoming. She visited Indian friends near the trading post. The army officers there knew her and gave her gifts. From Fort Laramie she traveled to Fort Bridger, in what is now southwestern Wyoming where she visited a Ute friend, the wife of Jim Bridger.

Bridger, sometimes called "the Daniel Boone of the Rockies," had built Fort Bridger in the early 1840s. It was the first place after Fort Laramie where emigrants to the Far West on the Oregon Trail could repair their wagons, let their horses and cattle rest, and purchase supplies. And there were many thousands of emigrants especially after the discovery of gold in California in 1849. So it was a good trading post for the Indians, too. Soon a branch of the American Fur Company was located there.

How long Sacagawea stayed with Mrs. Bridger is not known. But there were Shoshones living in that area and she seems to have joined them. A Wyoming pioneer, Charles Bocker, wrote that he had purchased "a pair of moccasins from Sacajawea in 1865 when she came down from her lodge." She lived north of Fort Bridger with other Indians. The following year he bought a buffalo robe from her, and in 1866 Bocker bought an Indian blanket.

When he was introduced to her, he was told that she had been on an expedition with white men. "Everybody all around everywhere knew it, and it was common talk. Bridger knew it, . . . the white men knew it, the Indians knew it." Bocker visited her, even learning a little of the Shoshone language. Trading posts needed interpreters. Eastman interviewed a man on the Wind River Reservation who had known several interpreters at Fort Bridger. His name was Edmo[nd] Le Clair, and he was part Shoshone and part French Canadian. When he was a boy, his father was in the employ of the American Fur Company at Fort Bridger.

Two of the interpreters employed there he remembered very well: Bazil and Baptiste. They both spoke English, French, Shoshone, and some other Indian languages. "Bazil seemed to be a leader of a small band of Shoshones," said Le Clair. "They lived part of the time near Fort Bridger, and part of the time roamed over the country south toward Salt Lake, Utah."

Le Clair remembered seeing Sacagawea also at Fort Bridger. Sacagawea, Bazil and Baptiste in the same place after an unknown number of years! Who recognized whom and when, no one seems to know.

"The family reunion was natural and a happy one," Eastman reported. His very brief account of her wandering is entirely different from Tom Rivington's story, but the end is the same—Fort Bridger.

Several elderly Shoshones whom Eastman interviewed said that they first saw Sacagawea or Porivo at Fort Bridger in 1868. As children, they had been there with their parents and grandparents at a special meeting called by Chief Washakie. Government officials—"Washington men," the Indians called them—were there also. Sacagawea unconsciously gave the boys and girls a good reason for their remembering her for fifty-seven years: she stood up and addressed the council— something a Shoshone woman had never done before.

Baptiste was not as well known as Bazil. Bazil was widely known as a fur trader, interpreter at Fort Bridger, and leader of his band of Shoshones. Who was he? Grace Hebard thought that he was the nephew whom Sacagawea adopted in 1805, when her brother, Chief Cameahwait, told her that their sister had died and had left a small son. If that is true, how did he find his aunt in St. Louis?

But Bazil did not look like a full-blooded Indian. Finn Burnett, who was a neighbor all the years Bazil lived on the reservation, said that his complexion "was very fair for a half-breed." We know that Sacagawea's nephew was not a half-breed, for his mother had never seen a white man. Wherever he was, Sacagawea's nephew was a full-blood.

One of Bazil's grandsons told Eastman, "My grandfather Bazil had light hair and his skin was much lighter than an Indian's. He had brown eyes." Eastman's conclusion that Bazil was the son of Charbonneau and Otter Woman seems logical. When and why Toussaint changed his name to Bazil is not known. It might have been because of his father's abuse of Sacagawea who had mothered him after he was nine years old or because of some confusion resulting from father and son having the same name. As both were in the fur trading business, the change of names seems sensible. Sacagawea herself followed the Indian custom of having several names. Half-Indian Baptiste did not change his; Bazil seems to have changed his only once.

Bazil "and his mother were much attached to each other," wrote Finn Burnett. Bazil was "exceptionally good to his mother," Eastman reported, "and she always called him 'son.' There are many instances among the Indians," he wrote, "where a nephew or step-son has been more devoted to the mother than the real son. This was the case in the relation of Bazil and his mother."

Sacagawea's years of wandering had ended. For the rest of her life she lived with Bazil and some of his family. After about sixty-eight years of separation from her people, except for a few days in August 1805, she was again with her band of Shoshones—this time, on the Wind River Reservation.

14

Sacagawea on the Wind River Reservation

PEACE-LOVING Chief Washakie, sometime near the middle of the 1800s, asked the United States Government for a reservation where his people could live in safety. Fewer than 1,200 people were in his band of Northern Shoshones. He wanted safety for them, not only from the warlike tribes being pushed westward by the great numbers of white emigrants coming into and through the area, but also from the white people themselves.

But the area assigned to the Shoshones by the government had no western boundary, so both the Indians and the white people invaded it. Again Chief Washakie made an appeal, this time asking for a more definite reserve. Wishing to show their appreciation for the aging Chief's friendship, government officials asked him and his chiefs to meet with them at Fort Bridger in 1868.

The Shoshones were there assigned a smaller area, but the warring chiefs and their tribes were still free to go where they pleased. The following year a band from a hostile tribe stole a large number of horses and killed thirty Shoshones.

Chief Washakie's next request included protection by United States soldiers and the organization of a strong Indian police force. He had to make several trips to Fort Bridger and to the Salt Lake Valley before the matter was settled in 1872. A few years later, the fort on the reservation was named Fort Washakie.

In May 1871, Finn Burnett was appointed Supervisor of Agriculture on the reservation. He lived on it for more than fifty years, except for brief intervals. In July, Dr. James Irwin, agent for the government, and his family were settled on the reservation.

Before September, twenty-four story-and-a-half high log cabins had been built. In a short time, Chief Washakie, with his family, and other Shoshones had arrived and moved into the new houses. The Chief soon earned the name "White Man's Friend," because of his loyalty to the United States Government.

His good friend Bazil and four generations of his family soon arrived. The oldest member, of course, was Sacagawea. Soon most of the Indians on the reservation referred to her as "Bazil's mother." According to tradition among the Shoshones on the Wind River Reservation, Baptiste, preferring to continue in the fur-trading business, did not join them with his family for a few years.

Sacagawea and Bazil were asked to live in the house nearest the agency, because none of the white people could speak or even understand the Shoshone language. The first interpreter employed there "talked very indifferent English" and had much difficulty translating into Shoshone the messages of the agent.

In 1925, fifty-seven years after the "Great Treaty" at Fort Bridger, Charles Eastman talked with several elderly Shoshones who remembered the meeting there. They remembered especially the presence of Sacagawea. If Indian women were permitted to attend a council meeting, they kept silent. But not eighty-year-old Sacagawea at the meeting at· Fort Bridger!

The old Indians' recollections given to Eastman were witnessed and certified by the official interpreter and by some other witness or witnesses. Here are a few of the stories that were recorded and sworn to be true. The first was told by a daughter of Chief Washakie, Engha Peahrora. Here is her story, translated into English for Eastman:

I knew Porivo or Chief Woman, the mother of Bazil. . . . I was very well acquainted with her from the time I was sixteen or seventeen years of age until she died. I first saw her at Fort Bridger.

In our roaming about, we came to Fort Bridger about once a year. . . . Her sons Baptiste and Bazil, with whom she lived, were employed as interpreters by the traders at Fort Bridger. At that time, interpreters were scarce in the dealings of the whites with the Indians.

In those days Bazil and his brother appeared to be leaders of a small band of Shoshones who roamed the southern part of Idaho, southwest part of Wyoming, and northern part of Utah. This band was on very friendly terms with the Mormons in Utah. Bazil and his brother, being leaders of this band, effected all the dealings with this band. I knew Bazil and his brother ever since I was a little girl. . . .

Porivo or Chief Woman, whom the whites call Sacajawea, many years afterward was well known among us, and I especially knew her very well. She spoke French, as well as her sons.

On our annual visit at Fort Bridger, she always was looked upon as the leader of our women. She appeared to be very well known among the white people of the Fort. I remember very distinctly that she was very much interested in the Treaty that Washakie was making with the whites at Fort Bridger, and I also remember that she was the only woman that spoke at the councils making the treaty.

At that time and sometimes afterward I heard that she possessed some valuable papers and a large medal which were given her long before by the government for some distinguished services for the white people. I have never seen the papers, but I have seen the medal worn by [one] of her sons at special occasions. . . .

When I first met Porivo or Chief Woman, I understood that she had come from the Comanche Indians. This must be true, because she spoke Comanche dialect rather than the Shoshone.

I remember when she was very old and living on this reservation [she told] about feeding some hungry white men with dog meat. I do not remember under what circumstances, where and when this happened. She often recalled little incidents of this kind that she told, but they are not clear in my memory.

She was the first person to introduce the Sun Dance into this tribe on this reservation. . . . Since then this Sun Dance has become permanently established here among this tribe. . . .

Later, in the presence of two men who spoke and understood both the Shoshone language and English, Washakie's daughter made this sworn statement for Hebard: "I knew that Porivo, or Sacajawea, took part in the council at Fort Bridger, because I was right there and saw her myself. She had a part in the meeting, and she spoke in the meeting. I know this, as I was there and heard her speak. . . . I am telling the truth." She signed her statement with her thumb print.

Of the many other Indians who made sworn testimonies to Eastman concerning Sacagawea, probably the most important were the son of Chief Washakie, the son of Bazil, and the two grandsons of Bazil. Dick Washakie knew her and her "kind disposition" when she was "an old lady at Fort Bridger" and on the Wind River reservation. "My father respected Sacajawea or Porivo very highly," he said, "above the ordinary Indian woman." Bazil and Baptiste were "close and intimate friends" of his father and were sub-chiefs under him. Dick Washakie ended his brief testimony with this statement: "The Shoshone Indians always believed very strongly in Sacajawea, and what was said about her in regard to her voyages that she had taken, and also what she said about her trips."

The testimony of Andrew Bazil, the grandson of Sacagawea, was long and informative. Only one sentence referred to her experience with the Lewis and Clark Expedition: "She used to tell with pride that somewhere she had fed the white people buffalo meat when they were very hungry, and spoke of them as having to eat dog after that. . . ."

Here is a part of Andrew Bazil's long report to Eastman:

I was about nine years old, as near as I can remember, when I saw my grandmother Porivo . . . for the first time. She was active, smart, and bright. She spoke French and she was free to go to the white people when we met any of them, especially at Fort Bridger. She was respected and looked up to by the Shoshone Indian women. As far as I know, my grandmother was always interested in the tribal affairs and often took part in the councils. . . . [He then told a good deal about the Comanches.]

When my grandmother was living, my father used to say to me, "You must respect your grandmother; all the white people respect her and honor her everywhere. Some day she will be useful to her people. . . ."

I have heard my father and others say [that] at the time Chief Washakie made a treaty with the white people at Fort Bridger,

Wyoming, my father and my grandmother both took part in it. They were influential in getting their people's agreement. I have seen a large medal worn by my father at special gatherings, and sometimes his brother Baptiste would wear the medal, because they thought a great deal of each other.

My father also had some papers that he carefully kept in a leather bag, which he said were very valuable. Later I learned that these papers were given to my grandmother by some great White chiefs.

My father was a very close friend of Brigham Young, the chief of the Mormons. In the early days, my father and his band of Shoshones often went to visit the Mormons, and Brigham Young always gave my father and his band plenty of food and clothing.

His father made an agreement with the Mormons, he said, to establish a school where the Shoshones could learn English and the Mormon children could learn the Shoshone language and customs.

My grandmother seemed to be very careful to keep the early part of her life to herself. There was only one person to whom she talked much about it, but told her always to keep it [secret]. She is my oldest sister. She is dead now.

Like Engha Peahrora, Andrew Bazil said that Sacagawea started the Sun Dance among the Shoshones. This important ceremony of the Plains Indians she had learned while living with the Minnetarees. She made Bazil its first leader. "Today, I am considered the leader of the Sun Dance," continued Bazil, "because my grandmother originated it."

(In recent years, the three-day Sun Dance held in late July or early August has been called "the outstanding social event" of the Shoshones in Wyoming. It is held near Fort Washakie.)

John McAdams, a grandson of Bazil, was only twelve years old when his great-grandmother died. "She was very old but very bright and gay," he recalled. He too remembered the silver medal worn sometimes by his grandfather Bazil and sometimes by his great-uncle Baptiste on special occasions. He knew nothing about the valuable papers that had been given her by Lewis and Clark.

"Very often," he said, "my mother stated to us children that her grandmother was noted among the whites and we ought to have some respect for her. I never gave much thought to it and did not ask what my grandmother had done that made her noticed by white people."

He did recall part of the preparation his grandfather said he had made in the early years on the reservation. He was going on a salmon fishing trip on the upper Salmon River and expected to be gone a month. So before starting, he took his mother and her tepee to the Indian agent and asked him to take care of her while he was away.

"Be kind to her," his grandfather had said to the agent, "because she was of great service to Lewis and Clark when they crossed the mountains."

The missionary who had been on the reservation for many years remembered probably the same incident, but thought that Bazil was going on a buffalo hunt, not salmon fishing.

Susan Perry was another Shoshone on the Wind River Reservation who was interviewed by Eastman. She had known Bazil and Baptiste years before she had seen Sacagawea. She also testified under oath:

When she [Sacagawea] first came to Fort Bridger she had gray hair, but she was a smart and active woman. She spoke five different languages: Shoshone, Comanche, Gros Ventres [Hidatsa or Minnetaree], Assiniboin, and French. She said that at one time she had lived with the Gros Ventres and that she had married a Frenchman. She further stated that she and her French husband had traveled with some white men toward the setting sun.

She spoke of some experiences when she traveled with the white people, but I do not remember what they were. I remember her once telling that she had fed the whites with dog meat when they were very hungry.

I remember during the years that we were living at Fort Bridger . . . she was perfectly familiar with the white people at the Fort. I mean that she was not afraid to mingle with them. During the time that she was with us, she was looked upon by the women of the band as the leader. The white people respected her. . . . Although she told many times of her wanderings, I cannot clearly remember all of them.

All of these Shoshone informants told Eastman something about the beautiful medal the white chiefs had given Sacagawea. Occasionally she wore it around her neck; apparently her sons wore it more often. James Irwin, teacher and missionary, also remembered the silver medal that Bazil wore "on state occasions." It was about the size of a silver dollar and had a gold rim around it. One old woman said that on one side was the head of God. James McAdams reported that Jefferson's head and his name were on one side of the medal.

The journals do not mention the captains' giving a medal to Sacagawea. But, similarly, Clark did not mention her or Charbonneau in his account of the journey to see the whale. However, both captains did report that on January 6, 1806, the two started with Clark and his party.

The captains generously gave medals to men who had done less for the Expedition than the Indian woman had done. To the Flatheads, for example, with whom the explorers spent two nights and a day after crossing the Rockies on the way westward, the captains gave four medals.

Memories of the Jefferson medal lasted for a long time. On the Wind River Reservation in the summer of 1953, with no thought of writing a biography of Sacagawea, one author (E.E.C.) of this book talked, through an interpreter, with a very old woman—Mamie Tyler. "I knew Sacagawea," she said, "when I was a girl and she was an old woman—like me now." My notes indicate that Mrs. Tyler had only dim recollections of Sacagawea's journey with "the white soldiers," but that she remembered distinctly the precious papers and the silver medal that they had given their young Shoshone companion.

If they did not give a Jefferson medal to young Sacagawea, how did the aged Shoshone woman on the Wind River Reservation get hers?

The papers that were mentioned to Eastman by several Shoshones were precious to Sacagawea because they had been given to her by "some great white chiefs." Her great-grandson, James McAdams, said that they were recommendations by "Big White Officers." Sacagawea always carried them with her in a small leather case, "so as to show that she was worth something." She gave the papers to Bazil, who put them in a wallet. They were buried with him.

Andrew Bazil gave Eastman permission to have the body removed from the grave long enough for him to investigate the papers. The wallet was in fair condition, but "its contents fell to pieces when exposed to the air, and none of the writing on the paper was legible."

Having finished his investigation, Dr. Charles Eastman wrote a report about it to the Commissioner of Indian Affairs on March 2, 1925. Here are his last two paragraphs:

> I submit the testimonies of three different nations, namely, Shoshones, Comanches, and Gros Ventres, the first in Wyoming, the second in Oklahoma, and the third in North Dakota. As there were no authentic records to be found after Clark had finished with them, Bird Woman and sons, we have to accept the tribal traditions, and when they corroborate so strikingly well, we must accept [them] as the truth.

> I report that Sacajawea, after sixty years of wandering from her own tribe, returned to her people at Fort Bridger and lived the remainder of her life with her sons in peace until she died April 9, 1884, at Fort Washakie, Wyoming. That is her final resting place.

Perhaps the disagreement over the time and place of Sacagawea's death would have ended years earlier if Eastman's summarized report to the Commissioner of Indian Affairs had been published sooner and had reached more readers. In July 1941, it appeared in the *Annals of Wyoming*. On June 1, 1976, administrators of the National Archives and Records Service were "not aware of any other journals or books which print the letter." Apparently a few individuals have been given a copy. (This writer [E.E.C.] was offered a copy after research on another subject in the Library of the Department of the Interior, Washington, D.C.)

But how many readers would know, as the Sioux investigator did, that storytelling around the winter fires was very important in Indian culture? It was important not only for entertainment, but for the preservation of history. How many would know that a youth desirous of being the tribal historian was carefully trained by his elders? Their tribal history must be accurate. Like the chief, the historian had a place of honor among his people.

Some passages in Eastman's letter are confusing in wording, but this paragraph is certainly clear.

> According to the statement of Mrs. Weidemann, a very intelligent woman, daughter of Chief Poor Wolf of the Hidatsa Indians, Charbonneau took both of his wives and their children to St. Louis a

year or so after Lewis and Clark departed from the village to St. Louis.

Was not Otter Woman the wife of Charbonneau who was on the boat with Henry Brackenridge when he was traveling up the Missouri from St. Louis in March, 1811? Mrs. Weidemann told Eastman that Otter Woman "was not well" when the explorers started up the river six years earlier.

Was not Otter Woman the Shoshone wife of Charbonneau whose death "of putrid fever" John Luttig reported in his journal on December 20, 1812? If Sacagawea had stayed in St. Louis with the two young boys, Otter Woman would very likely be "the best woman in the fort."

Four years after Dr. Charles Eastman had completed his investigation, James McAdams made to Professor Grace Hebard his certified testimony concerning his great-grandmother. It occupies ten pages in her book. His recollections give evidence that Sacagawea had greatly influenced the boy who, "for four or five more years," lived with her and his grandfather Bazil before he went to a school for Indians then in Carlisle, Pennsylvania. She died while he was there.

One detail in his recollections had been related to Eastman by other Shoshones: while she was traveling with the soldiers, she said, they became so hungry that they "killed horses for meat."

> She further told me several times . . . that one of the 'Big Soldiers' [she was traveling with] wanted to take Baptiste and educate him as his ward. Whenever she told this story, she would throw out her arms and then clasp them to her breast, saying "I wanted to hold my baby right here." In this way she opened up her arms as if to surround him and hold him closely so that he could not be taken away. . . .

> After the death of Sacajawea, how did the Indians feel toward her? The Indians never thought much about her work with the white men out to the coast, because the importance of that expedition had never been brought to the attention and minds of the Shoshone Indians, even though it was realized that Sacagawea had done an unusual thing and that the white men were under obligation to her. . . .

> There was another reason why the Indians did not exalt over her work—the fact that the Indian men did not like to see a woman go

ahead of them. Even Washakie himself and his followers did not desire that Chief Washakie should be placed on the top shelf and Sacajawea occupy a more prominent position in the esteem and appreciation of what [she] had done. This does not mean that there was any hatred or dislike by Washakie and his followers and other Shoshones, but it was a natural thing that the men should not rejoice in a woman's being a chief. . . .

Naturally, McAdams had heard about the Eastman investition of four years earlier. This second investigation prompted him to make some interesting comments in the last of his long testimony.

Our tribe all know and have no doubt that Sacajawea was the original woman from where she said she was—that is, a member of the Lewis and Clark expedition. Personally, I would like to ask, what is all of this fuss about? She cannot be buried in other places. She is here in the cemetery. She can only be buried in one place.

The story of her life with Lewis and Clark and among the Comanches and elsewhere was always the same and it was never any different—there was never any change or variation. She always spoke of the big waters—that is, the water that goes on around the world. I wish to also state that I know Mr. F. G. Burnett, who knows much about Sacajawea from his association with her and her family, for I at one time lived with him. . .

There is no fraud in the statement I am making to you, nor is there any fraud in this matter of identification of Sacajawea, the interpreter for Lewis and Clark. Fraud is not with the Indians in matters of this kind. They do not put up a story in order to have it startling and out of place. This I know from my long contact with the Indians, and particularly with the old ones. . . .

15

Finn Burnett's Recollections of Sacagawea

"FOR years, Finn Burnett was a fruitful source of information for the historians of the West," wrote Robert David in the Preface to his biography of *Finn Burnett: Frontiersman*. "At the time of his death in 1933, he was president of the Wyoming Pioneers' Association. He was universally respected for his honesty and admired for his achievements. Everyone who knew him felt his inner strength and hardiness of character."

Finn Burnett and Sacagawea were close neighbors and friends during all of her years on the Wind River Reservation, from 1871 until her death in 1884. (He was Supervisor of Agriculture on the reservation.) From Sacagawea and Bazil he learned the Shoshone language, and from her he learned almost everything he knew about the Lewis and Clark Expedition until years later. There could have been no better source of information for Eastman than Finn Burnett.

Sacagawea and Bazil, Burnett said, "were of invaluable service as interpreters to the agent during a long and important period of the reservation life." Sacagawea was of great value also, to Doctor Irwin, the head of the reservation, and to James Patten, teacher and missionary in the early years. "Into her house," Burnett continued, "and into their office at the Wind River agency, she and they were going many times a day. . . . It was she who kept the affairs of the office straight as to information that was to be sent to Washington."

Sacagawea and Bazil aided Burnett in teaching the simple facts and principles of farming. "There was not an Indian or a horse," he said, "that knew anything about farming." (To the Indians, horses were for riding and for indicating the owner's wealth.) Eventually, the Shoshones were able to plow, plant, irrigate, and harvest some 320-acres-worth of barley, wheat, and oats. Burnett attributed at least part of their success to Sacagawea: because of the "confidence the Shoshones had in Sacagawea and her son and their ability to tell the Indians what we wished to do, we got under way."

Until a few years before her death, Burnett said, Sacagawea looked as young as Bazil. She might have been his sister or his wife. Sometimes he thought that she looked even younger than Bazil. When she came to the reservation, she was remarkably healthy for her age. She was about five feet and five inches tall and had a somewhat light complexion for an Indian. Unlike most Shoshone women of her age, she was not fat. Her hair, as Burnett remembered it in 1926, was long and "slightly gray." She wore the usual costume of buckskin and a blanket.

After Burnett had learned to speak and to understand the Shoshone language fairly well, he went to Sacagawea's home to hear her tell about her experiences with the white soldiers. Often he had two companions: a schoolmate of years gone by and Mrs. Irwin, the wife of the agent.

Because of the interest the Irwins had in the Lewis and Clark Expedition, Burnett too became interested. "Mrs. Irwin was well educated," he said. She became so fascinated by Sacagawea's experiences with the Expedition that she decided to write the story of the old woman's life. Whenever Mrs. Irwin went to see Sacagawea—and she went often—she took notes for some future writing.

At the time Burnett became acquainted with Sacagawea, he had never read a book or even a magazine article about that first exploration. "During the period of the Civil War," he said, "I was not in a place where I could gain access to books, magazines or newspapers." Of course he knew a little about the Expedition from hearing people talk about what they had read concerning it, but most of what he learned came from

Sacagawea. When Eastman was gathering his information on
the Wind River Reservation, Burnett had retired and—tem-
porarily, at least—was in San Jose, California. Reached by
correspondence, he made a sworn testimony before a Notary
Public concerning what Sacagawea had told him about the
Lewis and Clark Expedition.

In the list of seventeen sworn testimonies in the Eastman
documents given to the National Archives by the Bureau of
Indian Affairs, that of Andrew Bazil is labeled "A−1," that of
Finn Burnett "A−2," that of John McAdams "B." Placing
Burnett between the names of the grandson and the great-
grandson suggests the high opinion given his testimony. Here
is the main part of it:

Burnett remembered that Sacagawea joined the party of white
men at a Mandan village on the Missouri River. She told me that she
saved the life of one of the leaders of the expedition [Lewis or
Clark?] near the place where they abandoned their canoes. She
spoke of the scarcity of food after the expedition had crossed the
Rocky Mountains, and said that the white men had eaten horses and
dogs—a most abhorrent diet to a Shoshoni. She said that she had
survived on roots that she had found and fish she had caught, but
would not admit that she had shared the horse and dog flesh.

She also mentioned several narrow escapes from drowning when
making the trip through the rapids and the falls of the Snake River
and the Columbia River. She said also that she saw quite a number
of "the people who live in the water," but could never get close
enough to speak to them. At every attempt to get near them,
they would get frightened and disappear. [She apparently referred
to sea otters.] She told me also of the rough water at the mouth of
the Columbia River and of the tremendous waves that nearly
swamped the canoes.

She mentioned the great fish that some of the Indians caught in
the "Big Water." The Shoshonis would never believe this fish story.
When asked how large it was, she said "as high as the ceiling of this
room and about as long as the door of this house is from the
hitching rack outside." This would be about 60 or 65 feet. They
would understand "the people who live in the water," as some of
them had seen seals on their visits to the Columbia River Indians,
but the whale story was "a lie."

She told of the hardships the expedition had experienced on its
return to the Eastern slopes of the Mountains and said that she had
guided Clark to the Clark's fork of the Yellowstone river, where
they had great difficulty in finding timber large enough to build

canoes. They decided at last to make two small canoes and to connect them together. With this craft they voyaged down the river until they met the other division of the expedition.

Whether she remained with the expedition until it reached the village where it had found her, I cannot now remember. . . .

Her son Bazile was a fine, portly man, nearly six feet tall and must have weighed over 200 lbs. His complexion also was very fair for a half-breed. He was crippled in one foot, and when walking, the toes only of one foot touched the ground. He and his mother were much attached to each other, and as before stated lived together until Sac-a-jah-wea's death. Another Indian who has been named as a son and identical with the babe she carried on her back on the expedition. . .was called Baptiste. He was a small man and had a complexion as dark as any full-blood Indian.

He made several visits to the Shoshoni Agency, but never took up residence there. . . . He was addicted to intemperance and when under the influence of liquor was a very quarrelsome man. He never lived with Sac-a-jah-wea while I knew her. She made her home with Bazile and his family and always called Bazile "son."

In September 1926, Burnett was back on the Shoshone Reservation and there gave a testimony about his recollections of Sacagawea to Grace Hebard, in the presence of the Interpreter for the Agency. He began by stating that he first came there on May 1, 1871, as "boss farmer." [He was then 27 years of age.] His testimony, five pages long, is Appendix B of Hebard's biography of Sacagawea. Some of it has already been quoted above. A few details can be added:

I remember very distinctly her telling me where and when she was taken prisoner and from her description of the place, I am almost sure that it was on the Madison fork of the Missouri. She and some other women and children were out gathering berries some distance from the main band, and she was captured with another young Indian woman, she told me. . . .

She and Bazil conversed in French, he said, and of course they did when any of the four "French half–breeds" on the reservation came to see them. "Other Indians told me," Burnett continued, "that Sacajawea was conversant in several different languages."

Sacajawea was always modest and never bragging about her being helpful to Lewis and Clark. Sometimes we had difficulty in inducing her to talk on account of her diffidence. . . .

Burnett told, in more detail than in his testimony for Eastman, his recollections of Mrs. Irwin's manuscript about Sacagawea and the expedition. It was on "legal cap" paper in a large roll:

The last time I saw it, it was kept with an autographed letter from President Lincoln to Dr. Irwin, for services rendered by him on the field of the battle of Shiloh. The last time I saw it, it was at the office of the agency, which was burned, I can't remember the date, but it seemed that a part of the records were saved. We hunted diligently for the letter from President Lincoln and the manuscript, realizing even then that they were very valuable. Some years after, at the request of Mrs. Irwin's daughter, I hunted for the letter and manuscript, but was unable to discover either one.

In a letter to Hebard dated January 22, 1929, Burnett wrote:

I have a vague memory of what Sacajawea related to me of her visits to St. Louis, Mo., and of Baptiste having been sent to school, and upon his return from Germany he told unbelieved stories of people who wore wooden shoes, and described great cities. The Shoshoni name for a German is 'Wo-be-namp-Tike,' 'Wooden-Shoe-White-Man.'

If Sacajawea ever married a Comanche, I do not remember it. She always spoke of Charbonneau as being a bad man who would strike her on the least provocation. She thought a lot of Clark who on the Lewis and Clark expedition took her part and would not allow Charbonneau to abuse her. I am disappointed in not being able to relate more of the history of this wonderful woman, but remember that it has been 45 years since she passed away.

The most interesting and the fullest account of Burnett's recollections of Sacagawea may be found in Robert David's biography. In the Preface, David says: "In his later years Burnett related at length his personal experiences to his granddaughter, who set them down verbatim. It was from these extensive notes" that David wrote "the full story of Burnett's adventurous life. . . ."

In David's seven pages about Sacagawea, there is of course repetition and enlargement of earlier reports. On the third page is an incident that some readers were probably surprised not to have read before:

Finally, when they had managed to contact these Indians [the Shoshones], Sacajawea was overjoyed to discover her brother, Chief Cameahwait, among them. After a joyful reunion, she began to talk the language of her childhood again, and told him that the white men wished to cross the mountains. She explained that Lewis and Clark needed Shoshones for guides, and a sufficient number of ponies to transport their provisions and equipment to the head-waters of the Columbia River.

The rest of that story is not entirely true—but Burnett had remembered the part quoted for about forty-five years!

Another part of his previous reports is enlarged:

They encountered terrible hardships on the western slope. Game was very scarce, and soon the party was reduced to the extremity of eating the dogs which had followed the expedition. The Shoshoni guides were disgusted with the white men for consuming these animals, stating that they would rather die of hunger than eat these camp scavengers.

In David's book, Burnett's account of Sacagawea's story of the "great fish" and the "seals" is longer and made amusing by repeating the questions and Sacagawea's answers. "They could believe that people lived under water, but not that fish could grow to be as huge" as the one she had described. There were other Shoshones at the agency who had seen seals. " 'Those people come right out of the water to walk on the beach,' they would declare. 'They walked like people, but they had long tails.' " When the expedition reached the mouth of the Columbia, Sacagawea said, the water was so rough that the men had great difficulty in keeping their light boats afloat.

Her account of the size of the waves was also disbelieved by her listeners.

Finn was never able to establish definitely the number of years which elapsed between the date of the Lewis and Clark expedition and that of her return to the Shoshoni.

Her tribe claimed relationship to the Comanche, and it is an established fact that both tribes spoke the same language. . . . Thus, it was very possible that she may have visited with the Comanche for a number of years, as her remarks would lead one to believe. At any rate, it was generally known that she was living with her son, Bazil, and his family near Fort Bridger in 1868, at the time that the treaty was made which ceded the present Shoshoni reservation to the Shoshoni Indians.

A few years after the death of Sacagawea in 1884,

some controversy arose over an Indian woman who was buried somewhere in Dakota, and who had been the wife of Charbonneau, and who was therefore supposed to be Sacajawea. She probably had been a girl companion, one of those Shoshoni children who had been stolen from their berry picking by the Mandans [no—the Minnetarees].

She might very well have been a wife of Charbonneau, as that Frenchman was a great marrying man. Sacajawea had been his third wife. . . . The fact that a Shoshoni wife of Charbonneau is buried in Dakota does not therefore establish her name as having been Sacajawea.

There were older men of the Shoshoni tribe in Wyoming who could establish the identity of the Sacajawea whom they knew on the Shoshoni reservation as being the sister of Chief Cameahwait. . . . There was never any question of her absolute identity in her own tribe by those who had known her from Babyhood.

In spite of Finn Burnett's integrity, there are naturally a few errors in his recollections. A date near the end of his testimony to Eastman is omitted here, because he (or the typist) was obviously wrong in stating that Baptiste's first visit to the reservation was "about 1884 or 1885." In September, when Burnett made his testimony to Hebard, he said "1874."

A few errors in geography may be due to his not being acquainted with the area west of Wyoming. He did not mention the Three Forks or the Jefferson River. The reader knows that the explorers traveled up the Jefferson, not the Madison River.

And of course "a lapse of memory" over the years would be natural for both Sacagawea and Burnett. Sacagawea came to the reservation sixty-five years after her return from what surely was the biggest event in her life. Finn Burnett made his two sworn testimonies about forty years after her death. His recollections recorded by his granddaughter were related "in his later years." He died in 1933 at the age of eighty-nine.

Surely it was a lapse in Burnett's memory, not in Sacagawea's, which caused him to say that, after the Expedition was divided on the return trip, "Charbonneau had guided Lewis with one portion."

Errors in naming Indian tribes, found in each report of the recollections of Burnett, will be understood by anyone who has read the lists of names of some tribes in *The Indians of North America* by John Swanton of the Smithsonian Institution—for example, seven names besides "Minnitari" for the "Hidatsa"; seventeen names besides "Snake Indians" for the "Northern Shoshone."

If the old Shoshone woman who had a Jefferson medal and related, with only a few inaccurate details, the story of the first journey of white men to the Pacific Ocean and back again—if she was not Sacagawea, who was she? Was not Otter Woman the unnamed Shoshone "wife of Charbonneau" whose death on December 20, 1812, was reported in the journal of John Luttig at Fort Manuel? "Bazil's mother," Porivo (Chief), Wadze-wipe (Lost Woman), Pah-ribo or Pah-tive (Water-White-Men), Pohenive (Grass Woman), Sacagawea to her white neighbors and friends on the Wind River Reservation— was she not the young Shoshone interpreter for whom Lewis and Clark named the Bird Woman's River on May 20, 1805?

"I have never had any doubt," reported Burnett to Eastman, "that she was the real Sacajawea of the Lewis and Clark Expedition, nor did anyone who heard of her in our small group. . . ."

Eastman, for his part, was unequivocal; in his affidavit of March 1925 to the Commissioner of Indian Affairs, he wrote, "Porivo or Chief Woman and Sacagawea are one and the same person."

16

The Aged Sacagawea

WHEN Sacagawea made her memorable impression at the treaty-making at Fort Bridger in 1868, she was probably about eighty years of age. A Wyoming pioneer, Charles Bocker, had been introduced to her two years earlier. He judged that "she must have been an old woman of about seventy years . . . quite lovely looking for an old woman, and she could ride horses as well as any of them." She usually rode horseback to Fort Bridger every year, he added. (Did he know that in her youth she had ridden horseback across the Rocky Mountains, twice, carrying her baby on her back?)

Finn Burnett, in addition to the description of Sacagawea given in the preceding chapter, wrote elsewhere that she was "a very fine-looking woman and much thought of by the other Indians. . . . She was pleasing in appearance, a woman full of brightness and smartness. . . ."

Engha Peahrora remembered Sacagawea's kind disposition, her desire to do always what was right. "As far as I know," she said, "she always had kind feelings toward the white people, and they had a great liking and respect for her. . . ."

Both Sacagawea and Bazil were highly praised for the assistance they gave Chief Washakie at the treaty-making in 1868—praised by a well-known freighter of the period, Jim Faris. He first knew Bazil as interpreter for the Shoshones at

Fort Bridger. Faris told Eastman that Bazil "was a very useful lieutenant to Chief Washakie. He never claimed much honor, but it is a fact that he and his mother were the trump card when Washakie made the treaty with the United States in 1868."

Finn Burnett praised the two even more highly. He was not present at the treaty-making, but he must have heard a good deal about it and about other council meetings during the many years that he was Supervisor of Agriculture on the Reservation. Under ordinary circumstances, he said, a woman would not have been allowed to address a council, but Sacagawea "represented the white men as well as the Indians. There is no doubt that her influence was felt in all important questions that were discussed."

Chief Washakie was impressed by her intelligence and by her interest in tribal affairs that her great-grandson remembered from his boyhood. As an adult, McAdams knew Chief Washakie well. "Washakie and his head-men, or chiefs," he said, "thought that Sacajawea was a great woman."

The first years on the reservation were difficult for Chief Washakie and his twelve sub-chiefs, for several reasons. First, the Sioux and the Arapaho tribes were so hostile toward the Shoshones and the whites, wrote Burnett, that "the Shoshonis were unable to remain in the valley in the summer. So they would go back over the mountains." That departure would interfere with the farming that Washakie had planned for them. Bazil and his family and some others remained on the reservation during the summer.

The quiet, new life planned for the Shoshones was difficult for a wandering people, anyway. There was also the problem of the different bands of Shoshones becoming acquainted with each other and working with each other. The Lemhi Shoshones numbered about 400 when Captain Lewis visited them in 1805. They were only a small portion of nearly 1,200 of all the bands reported in the census taken on the reservation in 1871. The Arapaho and the Sioux tribes were much larger.

Finn Burnett had known "Washakie and other chiefs to visit Sacajawea's home near the agency and listen intensely to her conversation for hours." Sacagawea's wide travels and observation of different tribes, added to her natural intelligence, must have made her a valuable member of these discussion groups. The respect that both the Indians and the white people had for her was also of value. If she still had the calmness she showed when the boat almost capsized in the Missouri River, that calmness would be comforting to others. And so would her sense of humor which caused her grandsons, in 1925, to remember her as a jolly person.

Women were silent at meetings, but not when the matters were discussed around the fireside. Bazil was an eloquent speaker, with a commanding presence. And "he had a deep, musical voice." So what he and Sacagawea decided at home he presented persuasively in the meetings of the council.

The government always had firm friends in Chief Washakie, Sacagawea, and Bazil, "even though it did not always keep its promises." The influence of those three Shoshones "caused all the mountain Indians," said Burnett, "to remain peaceful during the Indian wars, and saved the government great expense and the lives of many pioneers. Wyoming is under many obligations to these three noble, true, and steadfast Indian friends."

Although Sacagawea helped to solve the problems of the new reservation, she had pleasures also in her old age. Her great-grandson remembered that she sometimes went to Utah to visit her friends among the Utes. One time the people at the trading post there noticed the Jefferson medal she was wearing.

"Porivo! Something grand!" they shouted. Then they prepared for her and the Shoshones who were with her a big feast, "in honor of her wonderful achievements for the white people when they were on their way to the big waters."

But Sacagawea remained unpretentious in spite of this unusual honor for an Indian woman, the recognition by white men, her consultation with Chief Washakie and his sub-chiefs about the problems of their people. Seemingly modest by nature, she also knew that "Indian men did not like to see a woman go ahead of them."

James Patten, who was teacher, missionary, and government agent on the reservation and spent the rest of his life in the area, made this explanation, in 1906, of the lack of publicity given to Sacagawea:

We out here live far from the centres of thought. We learn of many things we have the deepest interest in, but we are so far away that it takes so long to make an investigation, and we are so busy striving, not for wealth, but for bread and butter, we lose sight of the subject and eventually forget all about it. . . .

I believe most sincerely in the identity of the Shoshone woman.

The Reverend John Roberts, missionary on the reservation for fifty years, knew Sacagawea only the last year of her life. He had arrived at Fort Washakie in February 1883, appointed by the Episcopal Church to be the missionary among the Indians on the Wind River Reservation and among the white people nearby. He followed the first missionary and re mained there, after retirement, until his death in 1949, at ninety-six.

The day after his arrival, he went to the office of the agency to talk to Mr. Irwin, the government agent in charge of the reservation. There he was introduced to Bazil, "one of the head-men, an aged and a fine specimen of an Indian," able to talk English brokenly and to speak French. Then he was taken to see Sacagawea in her home. In his introduction, Irwin said something about her having been a member of the Lewis and Clark Expedition. Roberts recalled, many years later, that he was not impressed by the fact. He had come from Wales such a short time earlier that he knew little about the history of the United States. He was, however, impressed by the personality of Sacagawea, and by the fact that she was "wonderfully active and intelligent, considering her age."

In the morning of April 9, 1884, a close neighbor of Sacagawea heard that she had passed away. He hurried to her tepee. There he met Bazil, tears running down his cheeks. "My mother is dead," he said. She had died in her sleep. In the words of Roberts, "she walked alone and was bright to the last."

Her body was wrapped in skins and then carried outside, where the skins were sewed for burial. That afternoon the body was laid on her favorite horse, and Bazil led the horse to the cemetery. There it was placed in the coffin that the agent had his employees make for her. Bazil had asked Reverend John Roberts to conduct a Christian burial service for his mother.

Bazil asked also, his son reported to Eastman, that she be buried "in the white man's graveyard because she was a friend of the white people. . .at that time the Indians did not care to bury their dead in a white man's graveyard because they did not believe in the white man's religion."

"I was present when she was buried at Wind River," said Pandora Pogue in her old age, "and I went to the Shoshone cemetery and saw her buried. Everyone went to the funeral, both Indians and whites. I never saw so many people together at one time. . . ." (An estimated 1,000 attended the service.)

In the mission register of burials, Sacagawea is listed as "Bazil's mother. . .(Age) One hundred. . .(Cause of death) Old Age, (Place of burial) Burial ground, Shoshone Agency, (Signature of clergyman) J. Roberts."

According to tradition among the elderly Shoshones on the Wind River Reservation, Baptiste died the year after[14] his mother's death. In his burial, his family followed an old Shoshone custom: they carried his body into the mountains and let it down, by a rope, between two crags. (One writer tells an entirely different story about Baptiste's later years, his death, and his burial.)

Bazil died the following year—1886. A few friends wrapped his body in a sheet and a blanket and took it to a creek in the mountains. There they placed it in a new gulch that they had dug with their hands. His mother's precious papers were buried with him. In 1925, after his burial place had been found and the decayed papers had been examined by Dr. Charles Eastman, Bazil's bones were placed in a grave beside the grave of his mother.

Now, a stone column marks the grave of Sacagawea. On one side of her is a marker at Bazil's grave; on the other side, a marker for Baptiste.

Sacagawea "sleeps with her face toward the dawn on the sunny side of the Rocky Mountains," wrote Reverend Roberts. "Her grave overlooks the beautiful little Wind River Valley. . . . We see also the glistening waters of Little Wind River and of Trout Creek. . . ."

The view from her grave harmonizes with the personality of Sacagawea that Tom Rivington remembered many years after he wandered with her as a boy and she was past seventy years of age. This passage from one of his letters about her reveals something about her personality that is not revealed in the story of her life. It also suggests the most important aspect of the religion of the American Indians—their belief that there is a spirit in every aspect of nature:

She never liked to stay or live where she could not see the mountains, for them she called home. For the unseen spirit dwelt in the hills, and a swift running creek could preach a better sermon for her than any mortal could have done. Every morning she thanked the spirits for a new day.

She worshipped the white flowers that grew at the snowline on the sides of the tall mountains. She sometimes believed, she said, that they were the spirits of little children who had gone away but who returned every spring to gladden the pathway of those now living.

I was only a boy then but those words sank deep down in my soul. I believed them then, and I believe now that if there is a hereafter, the good Indian's name will be on the right side of the ledger. Sacajawea is gone—but she will never be forgotten.

Appendix A

Pronunciation of Indian Names

SACAJAWEA had been the spelling of the Indian girl's name since it first appeared in print in 1814. But a few decades ago, the Bureau of American Ethnology decided that the *j* should be a *g* because *g* is found in eight spellings of the name in the explorers' journals. We, therefore, have decided to use the preferred spelling, *Sacagawea,* in this book.

Sah-cah-gah-weé-ah is the accepted pronunciation. Sergeant Ordway's mention of "Sah-cah-gah, our Indian woman" makes us know the sound of *a*. The first three syllables mean "Bird," and *wea* means "Woman."

The name seems to have been given her by the Hidatsa Indians, who are always called "the Minnetarees" in the journals of Lewis and Clark. Their warriors had captured Sacagawea when she was a young girl. On May 20, 1805, the captains named a beautiful little river "Bird Woman River," in appreciation of her rescuing the medicines and other valuables when the boat they were in almost capsized.

The Hidatsa name for Bird Woman is spelled "Sakakawea." In the Dakotas, both the Indians and most of the white people use that spelling. They accent the second syllable and give a minor accent to the fourth syllable. There is no *j* in the Hidatsa language. (For more information about the name in the Dakotas, see Crawford in the Bibliography.)

Arapaho (A-răp-à-hō): a wandering tribe until they crossed
the Missouri River and settled in northeastern Wyoming,
where they were finally given a reservation.

Arikara (À-rĭk-à-rah): in historic times, they have lived chiefly
along the Missouri River in North and South Dakota.

Blackfeet: the most familiar of the 27 names given to the
Siksika tribe, whose territory stretched "from the North
Saskatchewan River, in Canada, to the southern head-
streams of the Missouri in Montana."

Cameahwait (Kăm-́ē-àh-wait): Shoshone chief and Sacagawea's brother.

Cathlamet (Kăth-lăm-́ĕt), Chinook (Shĭ-nook), and Clatsop
(Clăt-́sŏp): tribes near the mouth of the Columbia River
that were the kindest to the explorers in the winter of
1805–1806.

Cheyenne (Shĭ-ĕń): a wandering tribe, chiefly in the Midwest;
"in South Dakota, they were associated with the Cheyenne
River and the Black Hills."

Comanche (Cō-măn-́chee): "on account of their close linguis-
tic relationship it is supposed that the original Comanche
must have separated from the Shoshoni in the neighborhood of eastern Wyoming."

Flatheads: "widely so called because, in contradistinction to
the tribes west of them, they left their heads in the natural
condition, flat on top. . . ." Their scientific name is *Sālĭsh*. In
historic times, most of them have lived in western Montana
around Flathead Lake.

Mandan (Măn-́dăń): this tribe belonged to the Siouan linguis-
tic stock. When the Whites first knew them, "the Mandan
were on the same part of the Missouri River as the Hidatsa,
between Heart and Little Missouri Rivers." They were very
kind to the Lewis and Clark Expedition when they camped
nearby in the winter of 1804–1805 and also during the
brief visit on their return in August 1806.

Minnetaree (Mĭn-nē-tăh-ree): one of several names given to
the Hidatsa tribe. The word means "they crossed the
water." It is "said to have been given them by the Mandan,
from the tradition of their first encounter with the tribe on

the Missouri." They were kind and hospitable to the expedition in the winter of 1804–1805.

Nez Perce (Néz Pursé): "A French appellation signifying 'pierced noses.' " The Nez Perces "occupied a large part of central Idaho, and sections of southeastern Washington and northeastern Oregon."

Shoshone (Shō-shō-́nee): the Northern Shoshones (as distinguished from their relatives the Western Shoshones) "occupied eastern Idaho, except the territory held by the Bannock; western Wyoming; and northeastern Utah." The significance of the word *Shoshone* is not known. They were called by several other names. Five of the names mean "grass lodges" or signify "people that use grass or bark for their houses or huts." Eight of the names signify "snake people," "serpents," or "rattlesnake people." They were called "the Snake Indians" or "the Snakes" because of a general misunderstanding of their name in their sign language. "We are now very anxious to see the Snake Indians" (written on July 27, 1805) is the first reference to them in the journals. Next day, there is a reference to Sacagawea's "countrymen, the Snake Indians."

Wallawalla (Wäl-́lä-wäl-́lä): The name of the tribe means "little river." They lived "on the lower Wallawalla River . . . , and a short span along the Columbia and Snake Rivers near their junction, in Washington and Oregon."

Washakie (Wäsh-́ä-kee): greatly admired chief of the band of Shoshones in Wyoming, the band that Sacagawea lived with during her last years.

Yakima (Yāk-́i-mä): a Shahaptian tribe who lived "on the lower course of the Yakima River" in central Washington.

Chief source: John Swanton, *The Indian Tribes of North America*, Smithsonian Institution, Bureau of American Ethnology, Bulletin 145. United States Government Printing Office, 1952.

Appendix B

Sources

(See Bibliography for complete references)

Chapters 1–9

With brief exceptions, all the information in the first nine chapters comes from either the Coues or the Thwaites edition of the journals of the Lewis and Clark Expedition.

Indian traditions of the coming of Lewis and Clark can be found through references under Ella E. Clark, *Indian Legends,* in the Bibliography.

Chapter 10

Coues, pp. 1181–1184, and DeVoto, *The Journals,* p. 402.
Bakeless, chaps. 24–28.
Dillon, "Preface," xv; chaps. 12 and 13.
Coues, p. 190.
Thwaites, VII, pp. 329–330.
Dye, especially chap. 15 and p. 290.

Chapter 11

Taber, p. 8.
Harper, Vol. VI, pp. 540–548; Vol. V, pp. 123–125, 130–133, and 650.
Laut.
Sanford.
Creel.
Fuller, p. 62.
Hebard, "Pilot of the First White Men," and in last chapter of Schultz.
Schultz, *Bird Woman.*
Hebard, *Sacajawea: A Guide,* especially pp. 62–63 and p. 301.

Chapter 12

Anderson, pp. 6–12.
Brackenridge in H. P. Howard, p. 157.
Eastman in *Dictionary of American Biography*, Vol. V.
Brackenridge in *Dictionary of American Biography*, Vol. II.
Howard, H. P., pp. 156–157.
Luttig, p. 106. Editor's comments: pp. 11–25 and pp. 132–133.
Jackson, p. 317.
Vogel, p. 328.
Eastman, Selected Documents, Exhibit K.
Eastman, Letter-report to the Commissioner of Indian Affairs.

Chapter 13

Eastman, Selected Documents: Exhibit K, Mrs. Weidemann.
Eastman, Selected Documents: Exhibit M, N, and O–3, Comanche women.
Hebard: *Sacajawea: A Guide*, James McAdams, pp. 272–276.
Rivington in Hebard Manuscript Collection.
Bakeless, pp. 454–457.
Bocker's recollections of Sacagawea, in Hebard, *Sacajawea: A Guide*, pp. 186–188.
Eastman, Selected Documents: Exhibit C, Edmo[nd] Le Clair.

Chapter 14

Federal Writers Project, *Wyoming*, pp. 306–312.
Eastman, Selected Documents: Exhibit E, Engha Peahrora.
Brief sworn testimony of Engha Peahrora, in Hebard, *Sacajawea: A Guide*, pp. 247–248.
Testimony of Dick Washakie, in Hebard, *Sacajawea: A Guide*, pp. 246–247.
Eastman, Selected Documents:
   Exhibit A-1: Andrew Bazil.
   Exhibit B: John McAdams.
   Exhibit E: Engha Peahrora.
   Exhibit F: Susan Perry.
   Exhibit K: Mrs. Weidemann.
Eastman, Letter to the Commissioner.
Hebard, *Sacajawea: A Guide*, James McAdams, pp. 272–281.

Chapter 15

Eastman, Selected Documents: Exhibit A-2, F. G. Burnet (*sic*).
  Testimony given before a Notary Public, January 2, 1925.
Hebard, *Sacajawea: A Guide*, Burnett, pp. 230–239.
David, pp. 307–313.

Chapter 16

Hebard, *Sacajawea: A Guide:*
  Quotation from Charles Bocker, on p. 187.
  Quotation from Engha Peahrora, p. 247.
Eastman, Selected Documents: Exhibit Q, Jim Faris.
Eastman, Selected Documents: Letter from James Patten to Hebard.
"SACAJAWEA: A Symposium": John Roberts, "The Death of Saca-
  jawea."
Hebard, *Sacajawea: A Guide:*
  Quotation from Burnett, pp. 197 and 168.
  Quotation from James McAdams, p. 273.
Rivington in Hebard Manuscript Collection.

Indian Children's Story

IN the Wind River Reservation school in the 1930s, a highly praised teacher discovered that her pupils had little knowledge of the oral traditions of their people. Story-telling around the winter fires had almost disappeared. So she made a new assignment: each person in certain grades was to find some elderly person who knew a story, ask him or her to tell it, and then record it for the other students to hear.

This is one of the stories that were recorded:

Sacajawea was a Shoshone girl who lived with her people in the valleys of the Rocky Mountains. Out playing one day, she and her playmates heard a war-whoop. They started to run to their tepees. Sacajawea tripped and fell, and the enemy reached her.

Sacajawea was a beautiful girl. A warrior picked her up and threw her on his horse. He rode off and carried her to his own tribe, the Minnetarees.

She lived there for many moons. Traders came there to get beaver skins in exchange for gaudy knick-knacks. Charbonneau was one of the traders. One time he saw Sacajawea.

"Who is she?" he asked the chief.

"A Shoshone captive," answered the chief. "And she eats too much."

The Frenchman wanted to buy her, but the chief said, "We will gamble for her."

Charbonneau won. He made Sacajawea his slave, but her life was no harder than it had been with the Minnetarees. Later she became his wife.

When Lewis and Clark arrived at the Mandan villages, Charbonneau and Sacajawea were there. They needed a new interpreter. So they hired Charbonneau. He took with him Sacajawea and their very young son, Baptiste.

Lewis and Clark thought that Sacajawea could help them when they reached the Shoshones. When food was scarce, she found roots and berries that were good to eat. One time she saved the records and the medicines when a boat almost overturned.

When they reached the Shoshone country, she recognized her own people. She sucked her fingers, which was a sign of joy. She and one of the Shoshone girls threw their arms around each other. This was one of her playmates when they were captured.

When Chief Cameahwait came out of his tepee, Sacajawea rushed up to him and threw her arms about him. He was her brother. He and his father had pursued the Minnetarees but had been unable to overtake them. He told her that her sister had died a short time before. So Sacajawea adopted her sister's little boy.

The Shoshones sold horses to Lewis and Clark.

Many years later, Sacajawea returned to her people and settled in the Wind River Valley. She was cared for by Bazil. She lived to be very old.

Appendix D

Sacagawea Memorials

River

Sacagawea Creek, Montana, named by Lewis and Clark (Bird Woman's River), May 20, 1805, flows into Missouri River near confluence of the Musselshell, now known as Crooked Creek.

Mountains

Sacajawea Peak, Bridger Range, Montana.
Sacajawea Peak, Wind River Range, Wyoming, 1930.
Sacajawea Peak, Wallowa Range, Oregon.

Lakes

Lake Sacajawea, Longview, Washington.
Lake Sakakawea, North Dakota.

Statues

Louisiana Purchase Exposition Grounds, St. Louis, 1904, by Bruno
 Louis Zimm.
City Park, Portland, Oregon, 1905 by Alice Cooper.
Indian girl pointing the way for Lewis and Clark, 1910, by Cyrus
 Edwin Dallin.
Bronze of Sakakawea erected in 1910 by Federated Club Women
 and school children of North Dakota, Capitol grounds, Bismarck,
 North Dakota, by Leonard Crunelle.
Group, Sacagawea with Lewis and Clark at:
 Charlottesville, Virginia
 Oklahoma City, Oklahoma
 Helena, Montana
 Salem, Oregon, by Leo Friedlander, October 1938.
 Fort Benton, Montana, Park, 1976 Bicentennial.
Montana Historical Society Gallery, Helena, Montana.
Sacagawea statue by sculptor Harry Jackson, Plains Indian Museum,
 Buffalo Bill Historical Center at Cody, Wyoming, dedicated July 4,
 1980.

Markers

Concrete headstone with bronze plaque, Sacagawea grave on Shoshone Reservation, near Landers, Wyoming, 1909. Headstone
donated by Mr. H. E. Wadsworth, the Indian Agent, and Mr. Tim-
othy H. Burke.

Interstate Montana-Idaho Sacajawea National Monument, at sum-
mit of Lemhi Pass 7500 feet, on boundary between states, 1932.

Sacajawea Recreation Division of the Salmon and Beaverhead
National Forests, 1932.

Bronze tablet, on wall of Bishop Randall Chapel, Shoshone Cemetery, Wyoming, 1931.

Granite Marker, Shoshone Cemetery, for Bazil, Baptiste and
Baptiste's daughter, Barbara Meyers, 1932.

Plaque placed at Sacagawea's grave by National Historic Society,
Daughters of the American Revolution, 1963.

Marker, beside U.S. Highway No. 287 pointing toward grave, by
Wyoming Historical Landmark Commission, September 26, 1941,
great-granddaughters of Sacagawea participated.

Boulder with bronze tablet, honoring meeting place of Sacagawea
and her brother, Chief Cameahwait, near confluence of Horse
Prairie and Red Rock Creeks, Armstead, Montana, 1914, by
Montana Daughters of the American Revolution.

Boulder and Brass Tablet, by Daughters of the American Revolution, near Three Forks, Montana, 1914.

Two monuments near presumed birthplace of Sacagawea, Salmon,
Idaho.

Sakakawea, near Mobridge, South Dakota.

Paintings

"Sacajawea on Indian Pony," with child in papoose cradle, by Henry
Altman, 1905.

"Sacajawea," library building, State University of Montana by
Edward Samuel Paxson, 1906. Mural, "Lewis and Clark at Three
Forks," by Edward Samuel Paxson, Capitol, Helena, Montana,
1912.

"The Shoshonis naming Sacajawea," by William P. Dunlap, 1925.

Mural, Capitol, Helena, Montana by Charles M. Russell, representing meeting of Sacagawea and her brother, Chief Cameahwait.

Sacagawea, by N. C. Wyeth, Bettman Archive.

Music

"Sacajawea," intermezzo, by Rollin Bond, a bandmaster, New York
City.

"Sacajawea," song, lyrics by Porter Bryan Coolidge, of Lander,
Wyoming, and music by Frederick Bouthroyd, Leicester, England, 1924.

Cantata, "The Bird Woman, Sacajawea, A Legend of the Trail of the West," Toledo Choral Society, 1932. Text by Evangeline Close, music by William Lester.

Miscellaneous

Sacajawea Interpretive Center, Sacajawea State Park, Pasco, Washington, at confluence of the Snake and the Columbia Rivers, 1978.

Sterling Silver Set, Battleship Wyoming, 1912, gift from State of Wyoming.

Pageant, 1915, Beaverhead River Valley, near Two Forks of the Missouri.

Pageant, 1955, Three Forks, Montana.

Sacajawea Museum, Spalding, Idaho and in Washington State.

Airplane, "Spirit of Sacajawea," first flight, July 1927, over the Shoshone National Forest, Wyoming.

Sacajawea Club, Indian girls only, University of Oklahoma.

Schools in the states of Washington and Idaho named for Sacagawea.

Notes and
Additional Information

1. President Jefferson, on February 28, 1803, wrote the following letter to Dr. Benjamin Rush of Philadelphia. Dr. Rush was a leading physician and a professor of medicine at the University of Pennsylvania.

"I wish to mention to you in confidence that I have obtained authority from Congress to undertake the long desired object of exploring the Missouri & whatever river, heading with that, leads into the Western ocean. About 10 chosen woodsmen headed by Capt. Lewis my secretary will set out immediately & probably accomplish it in two seasons. Capt. Lewis is brave, prudent, habituated in the woods & familiar with Indian manners and character. He is not regularly educated, but he possesses a great mass of accurate information on all the subjects of nature which present themselves here & will therefore readily select those only in his new route which shall be new. He has qualified himself for those observations of longitude and latitude necessary to fix the points of the line he will go over. It would be very useful to state for him those objects on which it is most desirable he should bring us information. For this purpose I ask the favor of you to prepare some notes of such particulars as may occur in his journey & which you think should draw his attention & inquiry, . . He will be in Phila. about 2 or 3 weeks hence & will wait on you."

2. In 1783, Thomas Jefferson had asked General George Rogers Clark if he would be willing to lead an exploring party through the Far West. He was not interested.

3. Jefferson's request for Clark's captaincy was rejected by the War Department. To the disappointment of Lewis and the chagrin of Clark, the commission, when it arrived, proved to be that of a second lieutenant of artillery. Clark, however, on reassurance from Lewis that the command should be joint and equal in every respect, pocketed his pride and remained—by courtesy a captain. . . . It is to

the eternal honor of both men that in all the perplexities and stresses of that long journey the technical point of authority was never raised and that their personal relations were never clouded.

"The world will always, and rightly, call the expedition by the names of the two captains" (Ghent, pp. 86–87).

4. From Lewis's manuscript in the archives of the American Philosophical Society in Philadelphia, in May 1956, I [E.E.C.] copied the exact words of part of his entry of May 20, 1805: "this stream we called Sah-ca-ger-we-ah or bird woman's River, after our interpreter the Snake woman. . . ." A slightly different spelling has been written in red ink: *Sahcagah we a.* Today's most usual spelling *Sacajaweá* means "Bird Woman." This negates John Rees's belief that "Sacajawea was a Shoshone word meaning boat launcher or boat pusher."

5. Lewis and Clark's "Canoe Camp" of October 1805 is now a part of the Nez Perce National Park, which consists of twenty-two historical locations in the Nez Perce country.

6. From the Cascades of the Columbia River, the Cascade Range of mountains received its name.

7. When the great Canadian explorer and geographer, David Thompson, reached the mouth of the Columbia in 1811, he was disappointed to find the Pacific Fur Company constructing a trading post. The company had been organized by John Jacob Astor of New York. So it was indeed fortunate for the United States that the Lewis and Clark Expedition were the first to explore "the Oregon country" and to spend the winter near the mouth of the "Great River of the West." A long-time dispute arose over the boundary between Canada and the northwest territory. War was avoided when in 1846 a treaty fixed the boundary line as we see it on the maps today.

In 1853 a division was made establishing the Washington Territory north of the Columbia, the Oregon country south of the river. A beautiful Peace Arch extends with one foot on grass in British Columbia, the other foot on grass in Washington, and bearing the inscription: "Brothers Dwelling Together in Unity." (Federal Writers Project, *Washington,* pp. 39–44; Fuller, pp. 170–179)

8. Chief Shesheke (Chief Big White) and his family traveled to Washington, D.C. to represent his people and returned to his reservation in 1809.

9. The other five are Mary Lyon, Dorothea Lynde Dix, Susan B. Anthony, Harriet Beecher Stowe, and Frances Willard.

10. Great Britain and the United States formally declared war in June 1812. Fighting in William Clark's area lasted until news reached the American West that a peace treaty had been signed in Europe on December 24, 1813. Clark was Governor of Missouri Territory at that time. For years after the war, he was busy making treaties with the Indians (Bakeless, pp. 431–432).

11. In January 1813, Clark wrote Nicholas Biddle that he would be in Philadelphia in February to see him about "the publication of the Lewis and Clark Travels" (Jackson, pp. 481–482).

12. Dr. Charles Eastman is not mentioned in Donald Jackson's long index to his book.

13. A second error in Clark's list was his report that Sergeant Patrick Gass was "Dead"; actually Gass lived many years longer than Clark.

Another surprising error was made by Governor Clark when he wrote the name of "Tousant Charbon[o] in Wertenburgh, Gy." instead of Jean Baptiste, his beloved "boy Pomp." Baptiste had become the ward of Prince Paul of Würtemberg, Germany, and had been educated by him in Europe. Later, in 1829, Baptiste returned to the United States and for a while guided European nobility on hunting trips in the West (DeVoto, *Across the Wide Missouri*, Boston, 1947).

14. Regarding Baptiste's death, another version by Harold Howard (p. 174): "he lived in California a considerable time, and on his way to the gold fields of Montana died in Danner, Oregon in 1866."

15. Additional testimony of Susan Perry to Dr. Eastman: "Sacagawea's name Porivo is a Comanche word meaning Chief Woman. . . . In connection with her story that she was coming back to the Shoshones . . . they took the Big Horn River and followed it to its source called Warm Springs; from there on they went over the [Continental] Divide and into the Snake River Valley. It was on this river, they found a camp of Shoshones. From these people, she learned that her sons were at Fort Bridger, Wyoming. . . . the last time I saw the medal, it was in the possession of my sister, wife of Baptiste . . . I have heard it was buried with one of Baptiste's sons."

16. June Reading, San Diego historian, published the article "Wind River Scout—Baptiste Charbonneau" in the *San Diego Historical Society Quarterly* (1965) that stated he was enlisted in 1846 to guide the Mormon Battalion from Council Bluffs, Iowa through Santa Fe, New Mexico to its destination in San Diego County, January 1847, under the command of U.S. Army Colonel Philip St. George Cooke to strengthen U.S. Army forces then at war with Mexico.

After the war, Baptiste, the most intelligent and best educated man available, was appointed alcalde (mayor) of San Luis Rey (California), becoming chief magistrate and establishing a large Indian school. Two years later he mined for gold in northern California on his way back to his homeland in Wyoming. In 1883, Baptiste Charbonneau attended the great Indian Rendezvous on the Green River of Wyoming, and he returned with his Shoshone tribe to their Wind River Reservation.

Bibliography

Books and Magazines

Adams, James Truslow. *The Living Jefferson*. New York: Scribner's, 1936.
———. "The Six Most Important American Women." *Good Housekeeping*, February 1941, p. 30.
———. *Who Was Who in America, Vol. II.* 1950.
Anderson, Irving W. "Probing the Riddle of the Bird Woman." *Montana: the Magazine of Western History* 23 (October 1973): 2–17.
Bakeless, John. *Lewis and Clark: Partners in Discovery*. New York: William Morrow & Co., 1947.
Chuinard, E. G. "The Actual Role of the Bird Woman." *Montana: the Magazine of Western History* 26 (Summer 1976): 19–29.
Clark, Ella E. "Captain Lewis's Montana Birthday." *Inland Empire Magazine*, 14 August 1955, pp. 8–9.
———. *Indian Legends from the Northern Rockies*. Norman: University of Oklahoma Press, 1966.
———. "Sacajawea Loyally Serves Lewis and Clark." *Inland Empire Magazine*, 23 October 1955, pp. 8–9.
———. "Sesquicentennial Remembrances: The Lewis and Clark Expedition as Seen Through the Eyes of the Indians." *Montana: the Magazine of Western History* (Spring, April, 1955): 31–39.
———. "Watkuese and Lewis and Clark." *Western Folklore* 12 (July 1953): 175–176.
Coues, Elliott, ed. *History of the Expedition Under the Command of Lewis and Clark*. New York: Dover Publications, 1965.
Crawford, Helen. "Sakakawea." *North Dakota Historical Quarterly* 1 (April 1927): 5–15.
Cutright, Paul Russell. *A History of the Lewis and Clark Journals*. Norman: University of Oklahoma Press, 1976.
David, Robert. *Finn Burnett: Frontiersman*. Glendale, Calif.: Arthur H. Clark Co., 1937.
De Voto, Bernard. *Course of Empire*. Boston: Houghton-Mifflin, 1952.

————. "Sacajawea—Inspirational Maid." In *The Red Man's West,* edited by Michael Kennedy, pp. 119–120. New York: Hastings House, 1965.

De Voto, Bernard, ed. *The Journals of Lewis and Clark.* Boston: Houghton Mifflin, 1953.

Dictionary of American Biography. Edited by Dumas Malone. New York: Scribner's, 1935–38.

Dillon, Richard. *Meriwether Lewis: A Biography.* New York: Coward-McCann, 1965.

Dye, Eva Emery. *The Conquest: The True Story of Lewis and Clark.* Chicago: A. C. McClurg & Co., 1902.

Federal Writers' Project of the Works Project Administration. *Idaho: A Guide in Word and Picture.* Caldwell, Idaho: Caxton Press, 1937.

————. *Montana: A State Guide Book.* New York: Hastings House, 1949.

————. *Oregon: End of the Trail.* Portland: Binfords & Mort, 1940.

————. *Washington: A Guide to the Evergreen State.* Portland: Binfords & Mort, 1941.

————. *Wyoming: A Guide to Its History, Highways, and People.* New York: Oxford University Press, 1941.

Fleming, Thomas. *The Man from Monticello: An Intimate Life of Thomas Jefferson.* New York: William Morrow & Co., 1968.

Fletcher, F. M. "Sacajawea—Indian Woman." *Out West,* August 1905, pp. 113–125.

Frazier, Neta. *Sacajawea: The Girl Nobody Knows.* New York: McKay, 1967.

Fuller, George W. *A History of the Pacific Northwest.* New York: Alfred Knopf, 1938.

Garver, Frank H. "Lewis and Clark in Beaverhead County." *Dillon* [Montana] *Examiner,* December 10, 1913.

Ghent, W. J. *The Early Far West: A Narrative Outline, 1540–1850.* New York: Longman's Green & Co., 1931.

Hamilton, Charles, ed. *Cry of the Thunderbird: The American Indian's Own Story.* New York: Macmillan Co., 1951.

Harper, Ida Husted, ed. *History of Woman Suffrage.* New York: Woman Suffrage Association, 1922.

Hebard, Grace Raymond. "Pilot of the First White Men to Cross the American Continent." *Journal of American History* 1 (1907): 467–484.

————. *Sacajawea: A Guide and Interpreter of the Lewis and Clark Expedition.* Glendale, Calif.: Arthur H. Clark, 1933.

Hosmer, James K., ed. *History of the Expedition of Captains Lewis and Clark.* 2d ed. Chicago, A. C. McClurg & Co., 1903.

Howard, Helen. "The Mystery of Sacajawea's Death," *Pacific Northwest Quarterly* 5 (January 1967): 1–4.

Howard, Harold P. *Sacajawea.* Norman: University of Oklahoma Press, 1971.

Indians of Montana and Wyoming. Billings, Montana: Bureau of Indian Affairs, 1968.

Jackson, Donald, ed. *Letters of the Lewis and Clark Expedition With Related Documents, 1783–1854.* Urbana, Illinois: University of Illinois Press, 1962.

Josephy, Alvin M. "Naming the Nez Perces." In *The Red Man's West,* edited by Michael Kennedy, pp. 65–84. New York: Hastings House, 1965.

————. *The Nez Perce Indians and the Opening of the Northwest.* New York: Yale University Press, 1966.

Kingston, C. S. "Sacajawea as Guide: The Evaluation of a Legend." *Pacific Northwest Quarterly* 15 (January 1944): 3–18.

Laut, Agnes. "What the Portland Exposition Really Celebrates." *Review of Reviews,* April 1905, pp. 428–432.

Lowie, Robert H. *Indians of the Plains.* New York: McGraw-Hill, 1954.

Luttig, John C. *Journal of a Fur-Trading Expedition on the Upper Missouri, 1812–1813.* Edited by Stella M. Drumm. New York: Argosy-Antiquarian, Ltd., 1964.

McBeth, Kate. *The Nez Perces Since Lewis and Clark.* New York: F. H. Revell Co., 1908.

Peebles, John J. "Rugged Waters: Trails and Campsites of Lewis and Clark in the Salmon River Country." *Idaho Yesterdays,* Summer 1964, pp. 2–17.

Rees, John. "Footnotes to History." *Idaho Yesterdays,* Summer 1956, pp. 34–35.

————. "The Shoshone Contributions to Lewis and Clark." *Idaho Yesterdays,* Summer 1956, pp. 2–13.

Reid, Russell. *Sakakawea: The Bird Woman.* Bismarck, N.D.: State Historical Society of North Dakota, 1950.

"Sacajawea: A Symposium," *Annals of Wyoming* 13 (July 1941): 163–194.

Sanford, Martha Cobb. "Sacajawea the Bird Woman." *Woman's Home Companion,* June 1905, p. 5.

Schultz, James Willard. *Bird Woman: The Guide of Lewis and Clark: Her Own Story Now First Given to the World.* Boston: Houghton Mifflin, 1918.

Slickpoo, Allen Sr., Project Director. *Noon Nee-Me-Poo: Culture and History of the Nez Perces,* Vol. I, Nez Perce Tribe of Idaho, 1973.

Swanton, John R. *The Indians of North America.* Washington, D.C.: Smithsonian Institution, 1962.

Taber, Ronald W. "Sacagawea and the Suffragettes." *Pacific Northwest Quarterly* 58, no. 1 (January 1967): 7–13.

Thwaites, Reuben G., ed. *Original Journals of the Lewis and Clark*

Expedition, 1804–1806. 8 vols. New York: Dodd Mead & Co., 1904–1906.

Trenholm, Virginia, and Carley, Maurine. *The Shoshonis, Sentinels of the Rockies*. Norman: University of Oklahoma Press, 1964.

Vogel, Virgel J. *This Country Was Ours: A Documentary History of the American Indian*. New York: Harper & Row, 1974.

Webster's Biographical Dictionary. Springfield. MA.: G. & C. Merriam Co., 1943.

Wheeler, O. D. *The Trail of Lewis and Clark, 1804–1904*. 2 vols. New York: Putnam's Sons, 1926.

Manuscript Sources

Eastman, Charles. Washington, D.C. Department of the Interior. Letter. Dr. Charles Eastman to the Commissioner of Indian Affairs, 2 March 1925.

Eastman, Charles. Washington, D.C. National Archives. Record Group 75. Selected Documents Relating to the Burial Place of Sacajawea. Compiled by Charles Eastman.

Overholtz, Helen. Fort Washakie, Wyoming. Wind River Community Day School. "The Shoshones." ("1930's").

Rivington, Tom. Laramie, Wyoming. Grace Raymond Hebard Manuscript Collection, Western History Research Center, University of Wyoming. Letters. Tom Rivington to Grace Raymond Hebard, March 4, 10, 24, 1930.

Index

Adams, James Truslow, 84
Anthony, Susan B., 95, 102, 160
Arapaho tribe, 141, 148
Astor, John Jacob, 160

Bakeless, John, 112, 118
Bannock tribe, 119
Baptiste, Jean, 19, 20, 51, 56, 105, 108-109, 113, 114, 161; birth of, 14–15; Clark's offer to adopt, 82–83, 89–90; death of, 144, 161; illness of, 67; as interpreter at Fort Bridger, 120–121, 124; Pompey's Pillar named for, 75–76; at Wind River Reservation, 123, 125, 126, 127, 135
Bazil, 113, 114, 115; Burnett's recollections of, 132–133, 135, 141; contributions to 1868 treaty, 140–141; death of, 144; as interpreter at Fort Bridger, 120–121, 124, 140–141; moves to Shoshone reservation, 123; relations with Mormons, 124, 126; Sacagawea's life with, 121, 123–131, 135, 140–144; as son of Charbonneau and Otter Woman, 121
Bazil, Andrew, 125–126
Beaverhead Rock, 22, 23
Biddle, Nicholas, 87, 88
Bighorn, 63, 64
Big River. See Columbia River
Big White, Chief, 81, 82, 83, 160
Birdwoman's River, 17, 139
Bitterroot River, 37, 72
Blackfeet tribe, 119, 148
Bocker, Charles, 119–120, 140
Bozeman Pass, 74
Brackenridge, Henry, 104–105, 106, 130

Bratton, Private William, 56, 62, 67–68
Bridger, Mrs. Jim, 119
Burnett, Finn, 29, 56, 118, 121, 131; appointed Supervisor of Agriculture at Shoshone reservation, 123; on Bazil, 132–133, 135, 141, 142; on Sacagawea, 132–139, 140, 141, 142

Camas Prairie, 69
Cameahwait, Chief, 26–27, 28, 29–31, 72, 101, 102, 148; with Lewis over the Rockies, 32, 33–35; plans to leave Lewis for buffalo hunt, 33–34; as Sacagawea's brother, 28–29, 137, 138
"Cascades of the Columbia," 47–48
Celilo Falls, 46
Charbonneau, Toussaint, 13, 14, 15, 61, 62, 81; assessment of, by Lewis and Clark, 82; Clark's letter to, 89–90; decision to leave Expedition, 82–83; hired for Expedition, 15; incompetence during Expedition, 16–17, 19, 20, 33–34; as interpreter, 65, 72; journey to West in 1811, 104–105; land offered to, by Clark, 90, 104; later life of, 103–105, 114–115; marriage to Eagle, 113–114; marriage to Sacagawea, 8; during Sacagawea's sickness, 18, 19; wives of, 8, 104–112, 113, 114, 138
Chinook tribe, 50, 57, 148
Clark, General George Rogers, 9, 159
Clark, William, 101, 102, 159–160; appointed Brigadier General of

Louisiana Territory, 87; assessment of Charbonneau by, 82; contacted by Lewis for Expedition, 9–10; at councils with Minnetarees, 81–82, 83; on "death" of Sacagawea, 111–112; and frightened Indians, 44–45; hunting party led by, 38–40; journal and scientific research of, 57; journey to Pacific Ocean, 55–56; land sale to Charbonneau, 90, 104; letter to Charbonneau, 89–90; map making by, 57, 60, 64, 83–84, 89; medical treatment of Indians by, 62, 66, 67; offers to take Baptiste, 82, 89–90, 106; at Pompey's Pillar, 75–76; on Sacagawea's contribution to Expedition, 17, 18–19, 82; saves Sacagawea and Charbonneau during rainstorm, 19–20; search party to explore to the south on return trip led by, 71–79; search party to Salmon River led by, 30–31, 32, 34, 35. *See also* Lewis and Clark Expedition.

Clatsop tribe, 52, 57
Clearwater River, 41, 42–43, 66
Colter, Private John, 34
Columbia River, 25, 30, 40; Expedition on, 41–42, 44–48, 49–53, 61–63
Comanche tribe, 114, 148; Sacagawea among, 115–117, 137–138
Continental Divide, 24–25
Cooper, Alice, 94
Coues, Elliott, 88–89, 90
Creel, George, 98–99, 102
Crow tribe, 72
Cruzat, Private Peter, 30; Lewis accidentally wounded by, 80–81; on Short Narrows, 46; violin playing by, 11, 35, 47
Cut-nose, Chief, 68

David, Robert, 132, 136–137
De Voto, Bernard, 51
Drouillard, George, 10, 11, 12, 16, 70, 81; in Lewis' party on return trip, 79; in search party for Shoshones, 23, 24, 25, 26, 28

Drumm, Stella, 107–109
Dye, Eva Emery: on Expedition, 90–92, 102; on Sacagawea, 1, 16, 91–92, 93–94, 102; statue of Sacagawea promoted by, 94, 95

Eagle, 113, 115
Eastman, Doctor Charles, 2, 14, 110–111, 113–121, 123, 129–130, 134

Faris, Jim, 140–141
Flathead tribe, 35, 36, 148
Floyd, Sergeant Charles, 89
Fort Bridger, 119–120, 122, 123, 124
Fort Clatsop, 53–58
Fuller, George W., 99, 102

Gallatin River, 21, 73
Gass, Sergeant Patrick, 13n, 52, 70, 74, 79. 80, 81, 91, 161; journal of, 105
Gibbon's Pass, 73
Gibson, Private George, 56
Grant, Virginia, 94
Great Falls, 46, 71, 79
"Great Shoot," 47–48

Harper, Francis P., 88
Hebard, Grace Raymond, 109, 115, 121, 125, 130, 135; on Sacagawea, 97–98, 99, 100–102, 103
Hidatsa tribe. *See* Minnetaree tribe
Howard, Harold, 161
Hungry Creek, 69–70

Irwin, Doctor James, 123, 127–128, 132
Irwin, Mrs. James, 133, 136

Jackson, Donald, 111–112
Jefferson, Thomas, 83–84; documents from Expedition saved by, 89; plans for Expedition of, 8–9, 10, 11–12, 48, 57, 159–160
Jefferson River, 21, 73, 138
Jerk-Meat, 116, 117
Journals of Lewis and Clark: publishing history of, 87–89; Sacagawea in, 87, 88–89
Jussome, René, 12, 15, 81, 82, 83

Labiche, Francis, 30, 65
Lake Coeur d'Alene, 64
Laut, Agnes, 96–97
Le Clair, Edmond, 120
Lemhi Pass, 24, 31, 101–102
Lemhi River, 34, 35
Lewis, Meriwether: assessment of
  Charbonneau by, 82; appointed
  Governor of Louisiana Terri-
  tory, 87; contacted by Jefferson,
  8–9; gunshot wound of, 79, 80–
  81; preparations for Expedition
  of, 10–11; on Sacagawea's contribution to Expedition, 17, 18–
  19; scientific study of, 10, 57;
  search party over Rockies led by,
  32–35; search party to explore
  to north on return trip led by,
  71–72, 79–81; search party to
  Shoshones led by, 22–27. *See also*
  Lewis and Clark Expedition
Lewis and Clark Centennial Exposition, 89, 90, 93, 94, 95
Lewis and Clark Expedition: arrival
  at St. Louis, 83–84; on Clearwater River, 42–43; on Columbia River, 44–48, 49–53, 61–63;
  council with Salish, 36–37;
  council with Shoshones, 27–31;
  eastward journey over Rockies,
  69–77; eastward journey to
  Rockies, 59–68; at Fort Clatsop,
  51–58; isolated struggles with
  Indians, 79–81; Jefferson's plans
  for, 8–9, 10, 11–12; among Nez
  Perce, 40–42, 63–68; parties
  separate and reunite on return
  trip, 71–81; policy toward
  Indians, 11–13; preparation and
  training for, 10–11; Sacagawea's
  contribution to, 18, 19, 82, 84;
  Sacagawea joins, 13, 14–21; salt
  making on, 54; scientific contributions of, 83–84; search for
  Shoshones, 22–27; on Snake
  River, 43–44; thievery problems
  of 60–61, 80; westward journey
  over Rockies, 34–38; westward
  journey to Rockies, 11–33;
  winter camps of, 12–13, 51–58
Lisa, Manuel, 104, 105, 106, 107
Lizette, 106, 112

Long Narrows, 47
Louisiana Purchase Exposition, 93,
  94
Louisiana Territory, purchase of, 9
Luttig, John, 105–109, 112, 130,
  139

McAdams, James, 115–117, 130–
  131, 141
McAdams, John, 126–127
McBeth, Kate, 41
McNeal, Private Hugh, 23, 24
Madison River, 21
Mandan tribe, 12–13, 78, 82, 83,
  148
Marias River, 18, 71, 79–80
Matthews, Washington, 107
Minnetaree tribe, 12, 103, 110–
  111, 148–149; reached by Ex-
  pedition on return trip, 81–82;
  Sacagawea captured by, 7–8,
  20–21
Mississippi River, 83, 84
Missouri River, 16, 71–72, 73,
  76–77, 79–81, 83
Mormons, 124, 126

National American Woman's Suffrage Association, 94–95, 102
Nez Perce tribe, 149; Clark hunting
  party met by, 39–40; as guides
  for Expedition, 42–43, 44, 46–
  47, 61, 63–64, 70–71, 72, 74,
  79; time with Expedition, 40–42,
  63–68; tradition about Sacagawea's living among, 118

Old Toby, 64; as guide, 34, 35, 37;
  leaves Expedition, 43
Ordway, Sergeant John, 80
Otter Woman, 14, 15; confused
  with Sacagawea, 104–105, 106–
  109; death of, 130, 139

Pacific Ocean, 48, 49, 50, 54–56
Patten, James, 132, 142–143
Paul of Würtemberg, Prince, 161
Peahrora, Engha, 124–125, 140
Perry, Susan, 127
Pichette, Pierre, 36–37
Pogue, Pandora, 144
Pompey's Pillar, 75–76, 108

Poor Wolf, Chief, 14, 15, 104, 110–111, 113
Porivo. *See* Sacagawea
Pryor, Sergeant Nathaniel, 74–75, 78

Rivington, Tom, 118, 119–120, 145
Roberts, John, 94, 143, 144
Rush, Doctor Benjamin, 159

Sacagawea: alleged death of, in 1812, 106–109; assessment of, by Lewis and Clark, 17, 18–19, 82; Beaverhead Rock recognized by, 22, 23; Burnett's recollections of, 132–39; Cameahwait as brother of, 28–29, 137, 138; captured by Minnetarees, 7–8, 20–21; in Clark's party on return trip, 72–74, 79; among Comanches, 115–117, 137–138; confused with Otter Woman, 104–105; contribution to Expedition, 17, 18–19, 27–28, 72–74, 82, 84; death of, 109–112, 115, 116, 129, 143–144; Eagle on, 113–114; fictional portrayal of, 1, 91–92, 93–94, 102; at Fort Bridger, 119–121, 127; frightened Indians reassured by, 44, 45; historical books about, 99–102; as interpreter, 15, 16, 26–27, 64, 65; as "Janey," 51, 90; on Jefferson River, 22–31; joins Expedition, 13, 14–21; in journals of Lewis and Clark, 87, 88–89; last years of, 140–145; leaves Charbonneau, 114, 115; legend of, as guide for Expedition, 96–102; life with Bazil, 121, 123–131, 135, 140–144; loyalty of, to Expedition, 33–34; magazine articles about, 96–99; marriage to Jerk-Meat, 116; medal of, 126, 127–128, 142; names of, 139, 147; not a guide for Expedition, 16, 17–18, 21; Pacific Ocean seen by, 54–55, 56; "precious papers" of, 126, 128–129;

reaction to meeting Shoshones on Expedition, 27–28, 137, 138; reasons for wide travels of, 118–119; during river accident, 16–17, 147; river named for, by Lewis and Clark, 17, 147, 160; roots gathered by, 66–67, 68; among Shoshones, 119–120, 121–131; sickness of, 18–19, 49, 107–108; on Snake River, 44; statues of, 94–95; Sun Dance introduced to Shoshones by, 124, 126; time period between living with Comanches and with Shoshones, 117–119, 120, 137–138; at treaty council of 1868 at Fort Bridger, 120, 124, 125–126, 140–141; at Wind River Reservation, 122–139; winter camp activities of, 51–53
Sacagawea State Park, 44
Salish tribe, 36–37
Salmon River, 30, 35
Salt making, 54
Sanford, Martha Cobb, 97
Scannon, 11, 60–61
Schultz, James, 99–100, 107, 109
Shannon, George, 70, 87, 91
Shaw, Doctor Anna Howard, 95–96, 102
Shields, Private John, 23, 24, 67
Short Narrows, 46
Shoshone tribe, 15, 149; attacked by Minnetarees, 7–8; council of, with Expedition, 27–31; horses sold to Expedition by, 31, 33, 34–35; reservation problems of, 141–142; Sacagawea's later life among, 119–120, 121–131; sought by Lewis' party, 22–27
Sioux tribe, 141
Skitwish tribe, 64
Slade, Jack, 118
Snake River, 41, 42, 43–44
Spokane River, 64
Sun Dance, 124, 126
Swanton, John, 139

Tacutine, 116–117
Theft by Indians, 60–61, 80
Thompson, David, 160

Three Eagles, Chief, 36, 37
Three Forks, 71, 73
Thwaites, Reuben G., 89, 90
Ticannaf, 115, 116
Toussaint, as Bazil, 121
Traveler's-rest Creek, 70, 71
Twisted Hair, Chief, 40, 41, 64
Two Forks, 73
Tyler, Mamie, 128

Voorhis, Julia Clark, 89

Wallawalla tribe, 62–63, 149
Washakie, Chief, 120, 122–123, 124–125, 131, 141, 142, 149
Washakie, Dick, 125
Watkuese, 41

Weidemann, Mrs., 14, 110–111, 113, 129, 130
Weippe Prairie, 39, 42
Whales, 54, 55–56, 108, 109; Sacagawea's recollections of, 134, 137
Whitehouse, Joseph, 13n, 36, 89
Willamette River, 60
Wind River Reservation, 103, 109, 110, 116, 117; Sacagawea's life at, 122–139

Yellept, Chief, 62–63
Yellowstone River, 71–72, 73, 74–76, 78
York, 12, 16, 20, 47, 51
Young, Brigham, 126

Zimm, Bruno Walter, 94

LEWIS and CLARK TRAIL
1804-1806

0   100 MILES
0   200 KM

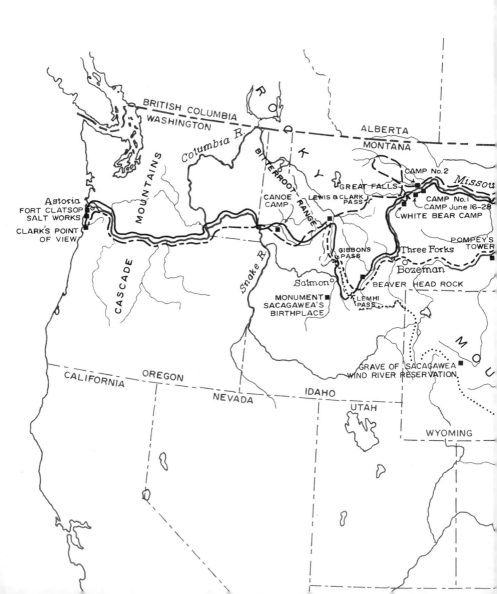

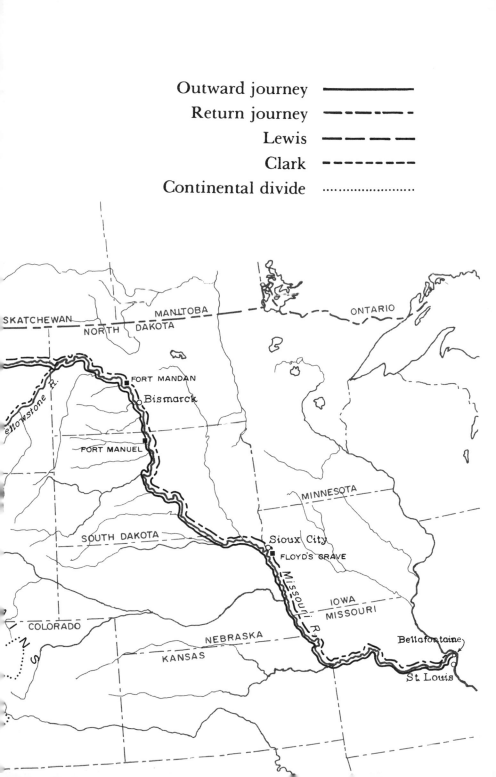

Outward journey ————————
Return journey —·——·——·—
Lewis ——— ——— ———
Clark ——————————
Continental divide ·····················

SKATCHEWAN

NORTH   DAKOTA

MANITOBA

ONTARIO

ellowstone R.

FORT MANDAN

Bismarck

FORT MANUEL

MINNESOTA

SOUTH DAKOTA

Sioux City

FLOYD'S GRAVE

Missouri R.

IOWA

MISSOURI

COLORADO

NEBRASKA

Bellafontaine

KANSAS

St. Louis